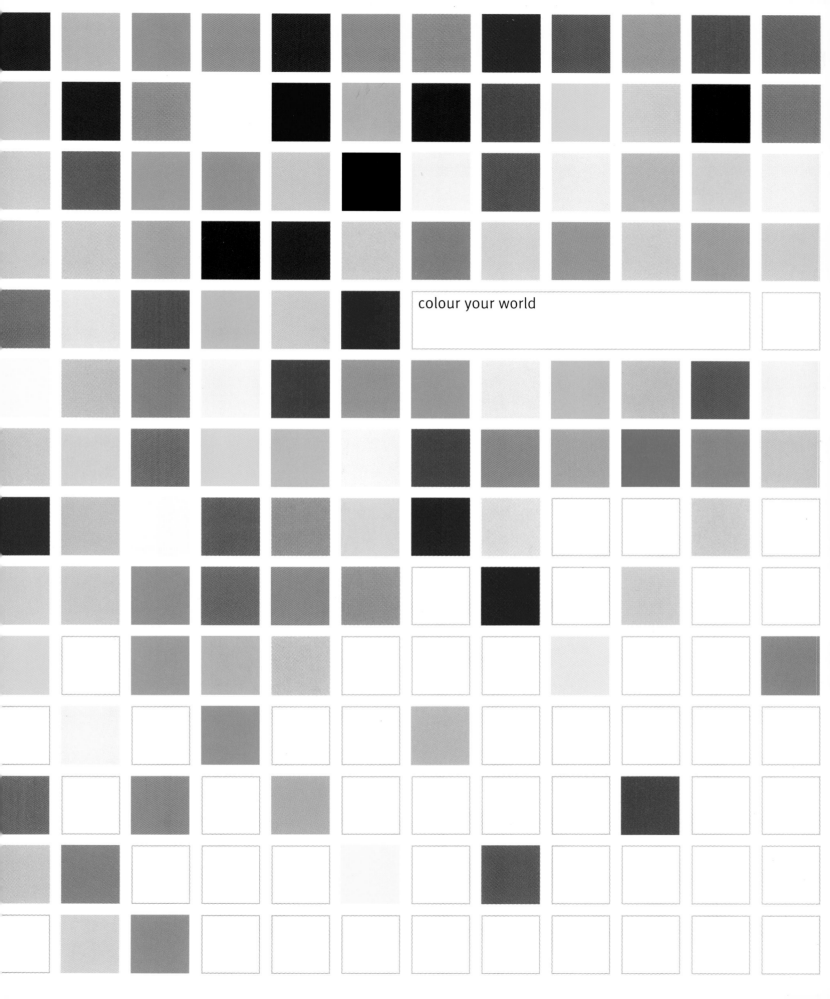

colour your world

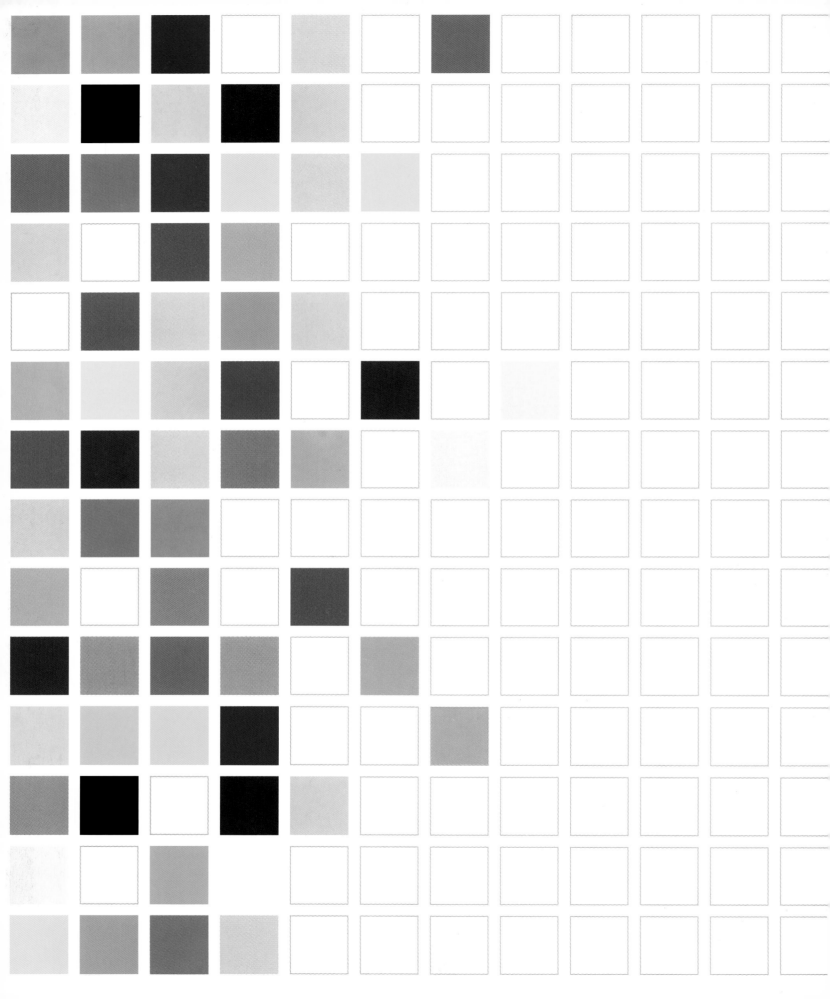

colour your world **Maria Flynn**

RotoVision

A RotoVision Book Published and Distributed by
RotoVision SA, Rue Du Bugnon 7, CH–1299 Crans-
Près-Céligny, Switzerland. RotoVision SA,
Sales & Production Office, Sheridan House, 112/116A
Western Road, Hove BN3 1DD, England. Telephone:
+44 (0)1273 72 72 68 Facsimile: +44 (0)1273 72 72 69

ISBN 2-88046-622-9

10 9 8 7 6 5 4 3 2 1

Book design by Brenda Dermody, Dublin
Illustrations by Austin Carey, Dublin

Production & separations in Singapore by ProVision Pte.
Ltd. Telephone: +65 334 7720 Facsimile: +65 334 7721

Acknowledgements

This book has been a vision of mine for several years now, but it could not have come about without a lot of help, and I would like to sincerely thank the following people for their efforts in helping me achieve my goal:

Natalia Price-Cabrera, Editor-in-Chief at RotoVision, for giving me such a strong, positive response from the start, and for all her work behind the scenes to keep things running smoothly and everyone happy. Brenda Dermody for such a beautiful design which is more than I could have ever imagined, and Austin Carey for interpreting my scribbles and producing such great diagrams. A big thank you also to Emma Smylie who was thrown in at the deep end, but did a great job researching the pictures and remained cheerful throughout a seemingly endless task.

On a personal note, I would also like to thank my two dearest friends; Lorraine, fellow dreamer, for her absolute confidence in me and her continuous support and encouragement – you are a tonic! And Alison, the perfectionist and total realist who drives me crazy, yet pushes me to achieve my best – you are always there when I need you and with your new-found editing skills I'll have to keep you on hand for a while. Finally but by no means least, thanks to Paul and Heather, who put up with my frequent absences and continue to support me in achieving my goals. You are both my source of inspiration and motivation, and you bring more colour to my world than I could ever have hoped for. I love you both, and this book is dedicated to you.

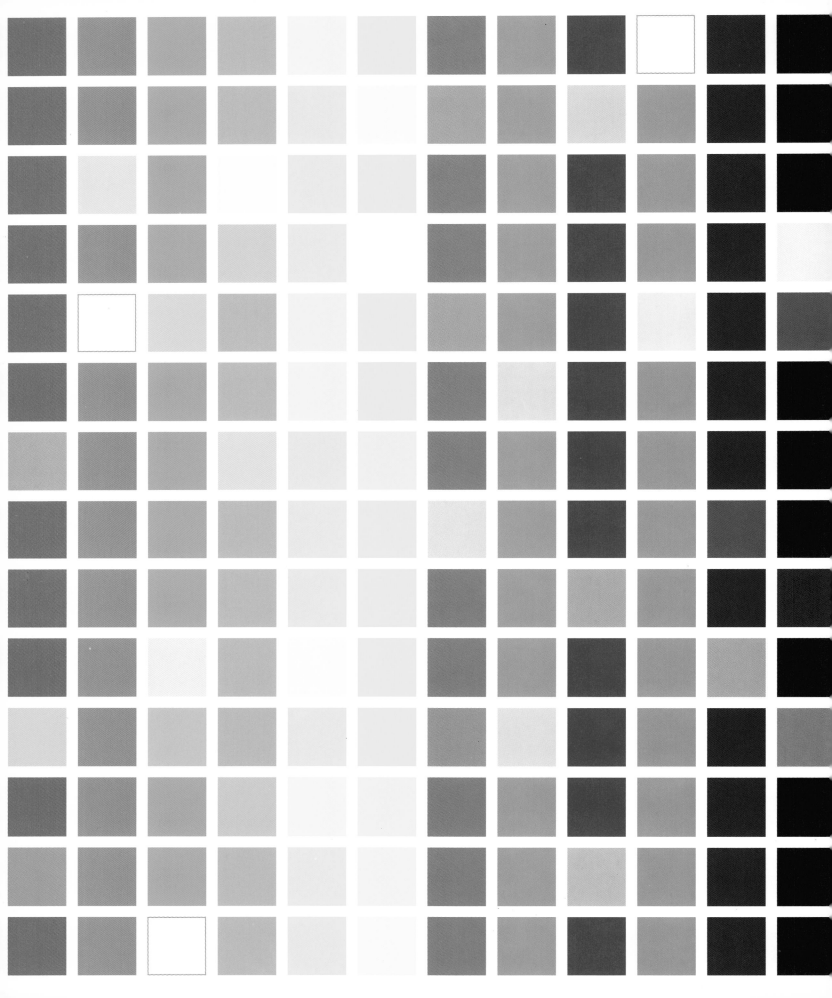

contents

Introduction

Colour is, without a doubt, the most powerful and exciting aspect of interior design. Skilfully used, it is possible to change the apparent height, width and overall shape of a room, and a change of colour can give your interior a fresh look or indeed, a radical change of style. A skilful designer will use colour to make unwanted features apparently disappear, or to highlight and draw attention to others. And there are also so many ways that colour can be introduced into a scheme, from applying it to large surface areas such as walls and ceilings, or adding small details by way of an appropriately placed bunch of flowers.

To the majority of people, understanding colour and particularly how to create successful, harmonious colour schemes remains something of a mystery. The few talented people that can create fantastic colour schemes are treated with great awe and admiration for their obviously magical talent. The general consensus is that you either have a natural flair for colour – or you don't. Although it is undoubtedly true that some people are particularly gifted in this area, these skills can be learned, and successful use of colour is something that everyone can master.

Having run interior design courses for a number of years now, lecturing to everyone from housewives to architects, I have seen an obvious need for a book that tackles the subject of colour in a complete way, and presents the information in language that is easily understood and enjoyable. This is the first book of its kind to be written for both the professional and the enthusiast, and why not, as this information will benefit anyone who is seeking a deeper understanding of colour and how to use it successfully in their interior. I have purposely avoided the use of unnecessary technical jargon and complicated terms, as these only reinforce most people's beliefs that they couldn't possibly understand such a complex subject. That couldn't be further from the truth, and I hope this book helps to dispel that myth.

Another gap that I hope to fill is in the fascinating area of colour psychology, which is only recently finding widespread acceptance in the interior design industry. Not only is this a vital consideration of any design scheme, but it also brings a new and exciting dimension to interior design. However, the real key to success is to combine this with a complete set of design skills, and the intensive section on colour psychology will show you how to do just that. It demonstrates how colour is used to affect moods and emotions, showing real-life examples where this has been put into practical use. It also examines the scientific evidence for colour psychology and looks at its importance in interior design. Clear guidelines are given as to which colours are appropriate for any given situation, so that you can apply it immediately.

I genuinely believe that good interior design can affect the quality of everyone's life, and anyone that can understand the basic tools can apply them to see immediate benefits. Whether you are decorating for yourself or a client, I sincerely hope that this book will help to build your colour confidence and that you can really use it to colour your world.

Maria Flynn

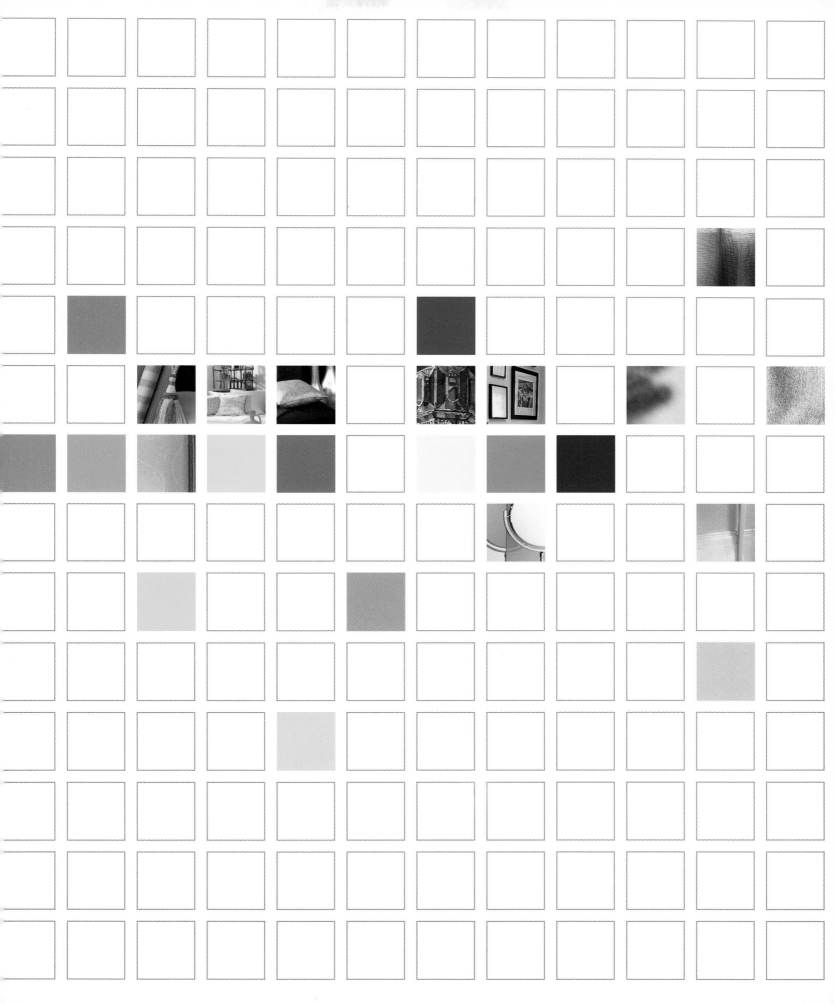

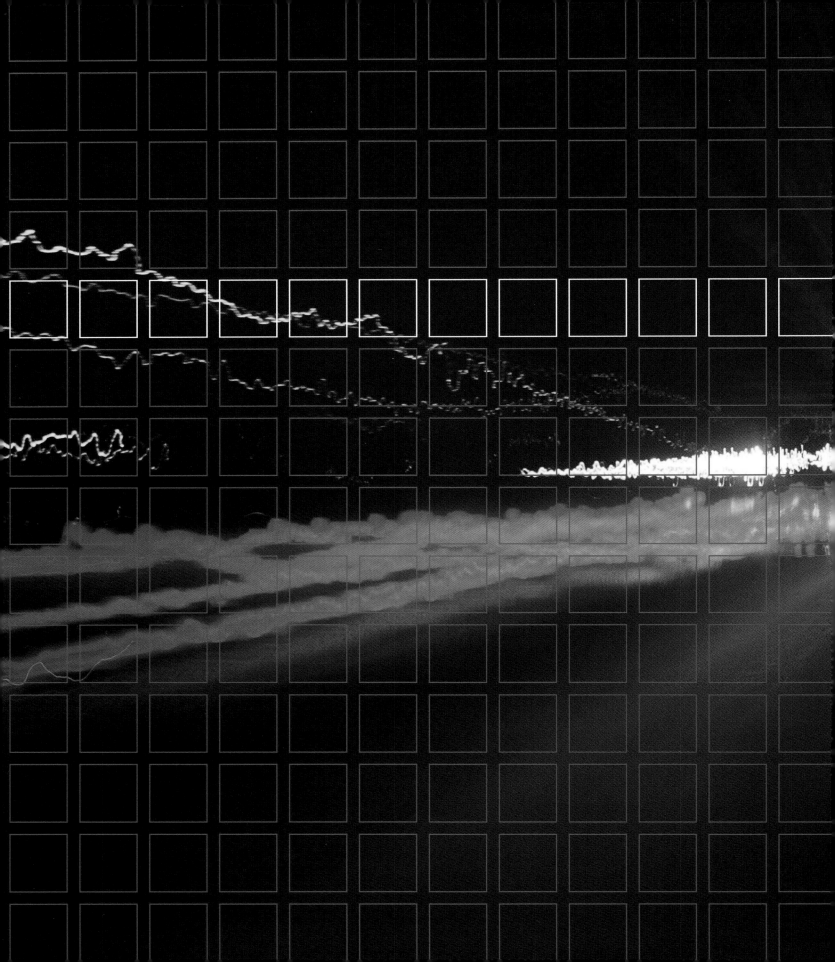

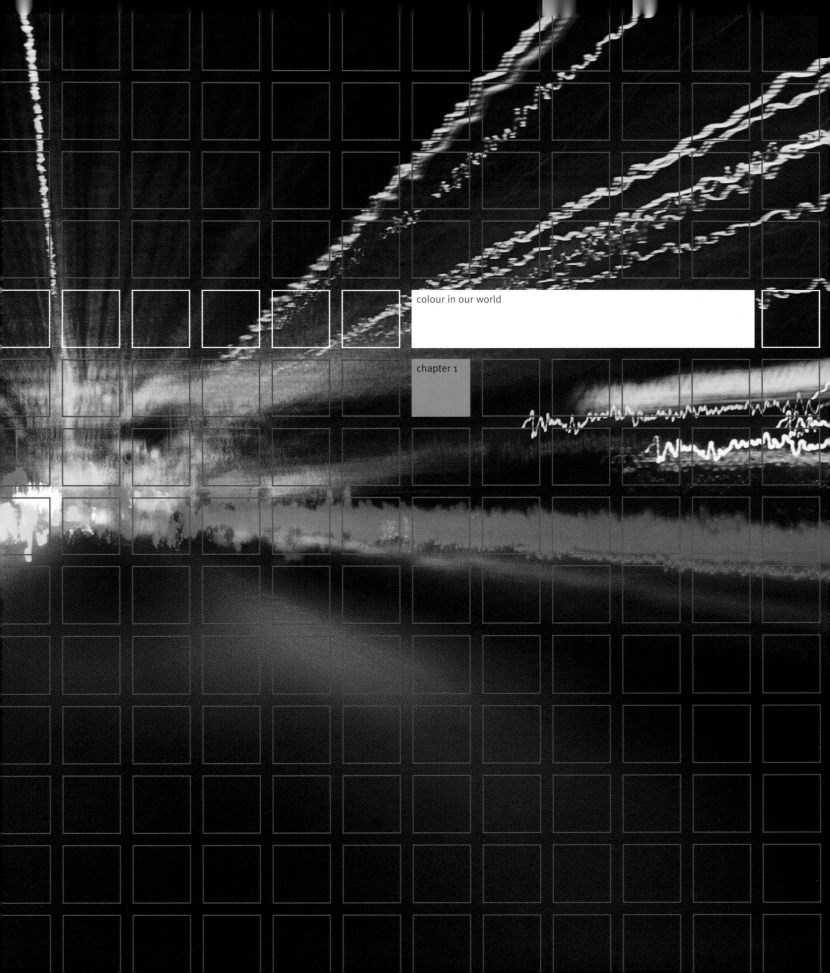

colour in our world

chapter 1

Like the air that we breathe, colour is all around us, filling our lives with its powerful energy and affecting our moods and emotions in ways that we often don't even realise. Also like the air that we breathe, we don't actually take time to think about the role that it plays in our everyday lives, and how much we take it for granted. However, evidence of the importance of colour is everywhere if we simply take the time to look around us.

Colour in history

Colour has played an important part in the history of mankind, for as far back as we can see. Cavemen mixed colours from the soil and plants nearby to paint murals on the walls of their caves. Of course, throughout the ages, methods of decorating progressed, as did fashion, and colours became more varied and more accessible as time went on.

In Ancient Egypt, the main colours used to decorate walls, floors and columns were red, yellow, blue, green, black and white. They adorned their clothing with precious stones and used embroidery and beading to add coloured details to collars. As we will see throughout history, the amount of adornment usually reflected the status of the individual and so became symbolic as well as decorative.

Still looking to the Ancient World, the Greeks and the Romans are famous for their classical architecture and design, but they were also lovers of vibrant colours and developed methods of decoration that we still use today. The Romans created wonderful wall murals known as *trompe l'oeil*, and had beautifully coloured mosaic floors and walls. These were often vivid in colour, and some wonderful examples still remain with us today in the ruins of Pompeii.

Naturally, access to colour in this way was limited to those who could afford it, and the more wealth one had, the more colourful one's life was. In Ancient Rome, the colour purple in particular was incredibly expensive to produce, as it required thousands of crushed snails to produce the dye. As a result, it became a status symbol to wear this colour, and at one time it was forbidden for anyone except the Roman emperor to wear purple. Quite appropriately, as we shall see in chapter 8, the colour purple represents spiritual leadership and so, symbolically, it was well chosen.

As mankind evolved and great cities and towns were established, trade routes were set up which allowed different cultures around the world to exchange all manner of treasures, including coloured gemstones, fabrics and dyes.

The Renaissance was one of the most exciting times in our history for a number of reasons, and colour seemed to explode into all areas in what seemed to be a celebration of life. During this time people began to question their religious rulers, and rather than looking to God for everything, they started to take responsibility for their own lives. Because of this, there was a huge interest in science and art, and the invention of the printing press meant that new discoveries and items of interest could be available to more people than ever before. For the first time in our history, it became possible for people to educate themselves, even the poor. This created a new middle class, and as people flourished and prospered, life for everyone became more colourful. Of course, the extent of decoration that you could afford (for your person and for your home) still reflected your status, and the new middle class spent large amounts of their new-found wealth trying to prove their worth. As many of them were still unable to afford the rich marbles, woods and elaborate draperies that were popular at this time, various paint effects were developed to simulate these more expensive items. Many of these decorative illusions were incredibly deceptive, and they have remained popular throughout the ages.

The Renaissance took place in the 15th century, so obviously a lot has happened since then, but it has all been built upon the firm foundations that were laid during that period of time. As we have advanced technologically, more and more choices have become available to us, in every area of our lifestyle. Now with modern production methods we have access to even more paints and dyes, and the colours we choose are only limited by our own personal preferences. Of course, the more expensive materials are still only an option if you can afford them, but many of the decorative techniques that were developed in the Renaissance are still used today, only now there are even more, and these are still under continual improvement.

In my design practice, I find it amusing when people see strong colours used in an interior and, regardless of the style, describe it as 'very modern'. Likewise, clients often ask me if I can recommend any of the 'new paint effects' that would be suitable for their purposes. As you can see, strong colour has been used to decorate our surroundings throughout the ages, and although paint effects and strong colour combinations are currently enjoying a revival, they have been around for almost as long as we have.

Colour as symbolism

Colour has always had strong symbolic meanings, and has been used to represent the pecking order in social and religious cultures for many centuries. We have already seen how the emperor was the only person allowed to wear the colour purple in Imperial Rome, and colour is used symbolically to represent spiritual and political hierarchy around the world. Religions in particular use colour to indicate position and to associate themselves with specific meanings. In the Roman Catholic Church, cardinals wear red, which represents leadership on a physical level, and the Buddhist monks of the East wear orange robes, orange being the colour that supposedly raises tolerance and strengthens will. We will look at the individual meanings of colours in more detail when we examine colour psychology in Chapter 8, but these examples should illustrate how religious groups in particular use colour to identify themselves with certain characteristics that each colour symbolises.

Many tribal cultures around the globe also use colour to represent mystical and religious beliefs in this way. The tribal members will generally apply colour directly to the body with body paint or tattoos, or use coloured stones and feathers to create decorative jewellery and head-dresses. We tend to associate most tribal cultures with the African continent, but there are also many similar groups living in the South American rainforests. The distinctive colours and designs that they use are hoped to attract blessings from the gods, repel demons and evil spirits, and increase fertility.

The Australian Aborigines and Native American Indians of today have mostly integrated with the modern societies around them, but they still each have their own distinctive art forms and ways of using colour. Most people would be quite able to recognise these types of art, and they have become very popular in the decorating industry, and are often used to create 'ethnic' interiors.

Within all of these various tribes and societies, some colours or designs would traditionally be set aside specifically for the tribe leaders or elders, similar to the example of the Roman emperor. If you think there is anything unusual or primitive about this, ask yourself why we choose to roll out the red carpet for visiting dignitaries and VIPs. By taking a closer look at our everyday life, we can see how even in our modern world, we continue to use colour to show which groups we belong to and our status within that group. At the highest level, individual countries are represented by a flag, and the distinctive design and colours will usually spark patriotism and loyalty within most people in that nation. This symbolism is particularly strong and is used to create a strong sense of unity by political leaders, particularly during times of war or major political campaigns.

Specific colours and designs are also used to identify certain professions through the use of uniforms, and many of these are recognised globally. For instance, in many countries in the western world, firemen usually wear red, policemen blue, and doctors and those in medicine are often referred to as the 'men in the white coats'. If any of us belong to certain clubs or associations, they may also have a uniform to identify members more clearly. One example that springs to mind is the Girl Scouts and Boy Scouts.

Football teams and clubs are also identified by their colours and designs. So strong is the urge to be associated with their sporting heroes, that many sports fans will pay large sums of money to keep up to date with the latest team colours and designs. Because of this, supporters of these clubs easily recognise each other and band together to support their teams. Unfortunately, this easy identification has also been known to cause conflict between opposing groups, sometimes resulting in actual physical fighting. Gang members in certain parts of the United States have also exploited this factor, where individual gang members will sport their gang colours, in the same way that the ancient tribes would have many years ago, as a call to 'battle'. Not a far cry after all from our primitive cultural and social beginnings.

Colour in our environment

Have you ever just stopped and seen how much colour surrounds us in the natural world and in the environment we have created for ourselves? Today, more than ever, modern methods of producing colours mean that we have more choices than ever before. This is also the first time in history that people around the world have equal opportunities to colour. Whereas in historical times, many people were denied access to some colours because of financial or legal restraints, nowadays colours can be produced extremely cheaply, and in our democratic society, the only limitations are the ones we choose for ourselves.

We have already seen how colour is used to reflect status and has specific symbolic meanings within different cultures, but it also has many other uses in our environment. Since the first cavemen painted on the walls of caves, bringing colour into our home and working environments has been extremely important to people throughout history. Spending time in harmonious surroundings creates a sense of well-being within us, and this is obviously the main focus of this book, but it is not just aesthetics, colour has very practical uses as well.

Colour is a universal language and is used to alert people to danger among other things. Red is the most advancing colour, and this is used around the world for traffic signals to stop cars from proceeding and for warning signs on the road. Yellow and black are used in many industries to caution us when the danger is not as strong, but care is still needed. Yellow and black hazard signs are evident throughout factories and warehouses, and indeed on many road signs in several countries. In large factories, pipes containing hazardous chemicals or gases are generally colour-coded to warn people of the contents. We use colour in this way to draw attention to hazards, but colour can also be used to attract us to advertising and signs.

In the natural world, colour is not only rampant, but it is essential to the survival of many animals and plantlife. Many animals use camouflage to blend in with their surroundings so that they won't be preyed on by other creatures. This is something that has occurred during the animal's evolution, whereby it matches its body colours to its surroundings, as an obvious way of protecting itself. By contrast, many hunters and fierce predators have strongly coloured markings on their bodies, which act as a warning to alert other animals of danger. In effect, this is nature's particular way of marking 'hazardous materials'.

Colour also plays an important part in reproduction. Flowers use their strong colours to attract bees and other insects to them, to aid their pollination and so their survival. Most animals use colour to attract a mate and this is something that we humans do also. It is obvious that many women wear make-up to look more attractive, but even without this help, when we become sexually attracted to another person, our cheeks and lips redden and become fuller. So you see, there is far more to colour than initially meets the eye.

Colour in our sayings

Have you ever noticed how many sayings we have that refer to colour? 'Red with rage', 'green with envy', 'in the pink', 'a grey area', 'the blues', etc.

The list goes on, and if you look at it again, you'll see that most of these sayings refer to our emotional state. Why do we use these particular colours? I mean, couldn't someone be purple with envy, why do we always relate the colour green to jealousy? One suggestion is that our subconscious mind is intuitively describing the colour of our aura, which is supposedly an energy field that surrounds all living things including the human body. The aura is generally invisible to the human eye, but some people claim to see it clearly, and describe it as a field of light radiating out around a person's body, which changes colour depending on the physical and emotional state of the individual.

The scientific community has scoffed at this for many years – and indeed you may think yourself that this is a lot of hocus-pocus – but recent advances in technology have helped to provide evidence to back up these beliefs. The Kilner screen, developed in London, allows us to objectively view subjects and their surrounding aura when they sit behind a special glass. And the Kirlian camera goes one step further by actually capturing on film an electrochemical emission that is emitted by all living things. What's more, the strength and clarity of these emissions are directly affected by the physical health and well-being of the individual. This is proving to be a valuable tool, successfully helping doctors to diagnose medical illnesses and treatments, and respected scientists from around the world are being forced to question their opinions. Then again, in the Eastern world, colour healing and the human aura are nothing new.

Colour healing

Colour has long been known to produce physiological reactions within the body, and this has been put to use in many cultures in colour healing. At the core of this practice, the Eastern mystics have long associated the seven spectral hues to the seven chakras, which are energy centres located on the body. Each colour of the spectrum is associated with a specific part of the body, and this is used to make a link between the mind, body and spirit. The diagram on the opposite page indicates the location of each chakra in the body and its corresponding colour.

In Western science, colour psychology is still a relatively new area, studying individual colours and the effects that they have on our physical and emotional states. Incredibly, there are striking similarities between the Eastern and Western colour associations, indicating that colour intuition can be quite accurate, and that colour truly is a universal language. We will take an in-depth look at this in Chapter 8.

So, now you can see how much we are all affected by colour, but you are probably wondering how exactly this can help you in interior design? Well, considering the obvious importance of colour in our world, it makes sense that we should give more care to the colours we choose to surround ourselves with at work and at home. Indeed, the colours we choose will affect our health and well-being, and that is why it is so important to select our designs thoughtfully. I hope that the rest of this book will help and inspire you to do just that, but first we need to take a deeper look at colour itself, and see what exactly it is and how it works. Let's explore the science of colour.

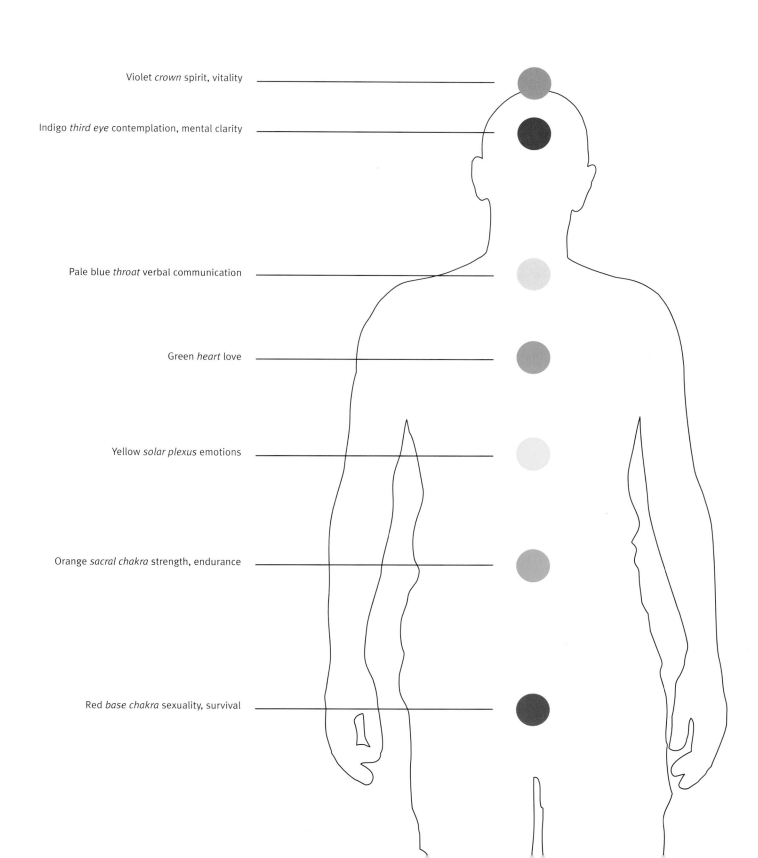

Violet *crown* spirit, vitality

Indigo *third eye* contemplation, mental clarity

Pale blue *throat* verbal communication

Green *heart* love

Yellow *solar plexus* emotions

Orange *sacral chakra* strength, endurance

Red *base chakra* sexuality, survival

the science of colour

chapter **2**

The science of colour

On sunny days, most people feel happier and show more of a spring in their step. This isn't just because of the sun itself, but because the sunlight intensifies all the colours that surround us and creates a more vibrant feeling. On days when the weather is dull and dreary, we often refer to it as a 'grey day', because the lack of sunlight strips the intensity of colour from the objects around us, and causes our environment to look dull and lifeless. What then is this relationship between light and colour? The simple answer is that without light, there can be no colour, or certainly the human eye cannot perceive it.

Have you ever had trouble finding your car in the evening, because if there is insufficient street lighting, it is hard to differentiate between the different colours of individual cars? Instead, each car appears to be a different shade of grey. The colour of the car hasn't changed, or the molecular structure. It is simply that in the absence of light we cannot visibly perceive the colour of the car. So then, what exactly is colour?

Technically speaking, colour is shattered light. White light (which comes from the sun) contains all the seven colours of the rainbow, and everything around us, including ourselves, either reflects or absorbs the individual rays of white light in different degrees. Sir Isaac Newton was the first scientist to make a study of

white light when he directed a beam of light through a glass prism in 1660. He found that seven individual rays of colour emerged on the other side of the prism in this order: red, orange, yellow, green, blue, indigo and violet. Furthermore, when he placed a second prism in the path of these seven rays, the colours mixed again and a single beam of white light emerged from the other side.

Since that first experiment physicists have arrived at a clear understanding of how light relates to colour. Simply put, light is made up of electromagnetic radiation, which is a form of energy. This energy moves at a constant speed in the form of a pulsation or wave, and each colour of the spectrum that is contained within the white light, has its own wavelength or frequency. (This is very similar to the way a radio works.) As each colour travels on its own individual wavelength, and the colours appear in order of their wavelength, this natural order of colour is always the same. Red travels on the longest frequency and requires the most adjustment from the eye, which is why it is sometimes seen as a stressful colour. Violet travels on the shortest frequency, and all the other colours are in between. Green travels on a frequency that requires no adjustment when it reaches the eye, and it is therefore restful. In science, the units used to measure the individual wavelengths of each colour are known as angstroms. For our purposes though, it is enough to know that red rays are known as longwaves and purple rays as shortwaves.

So far so good, but this still doesn't explain how we see colour. And if light contains all the colours of the rainbow, how is it that so many objects have different colours? The answer has two stages, so let's take a closer look...

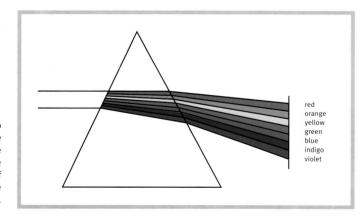

A simple way to remember the natural order of the spectrum is the phrase 'Richard Of York Gave Battle In Vain'.

red
orange
yellow
green
blue
indigo
violet

Firstly, let's try to understand how different objects around us appear as different colours. We already know that white light contains all the colours of the rainbow and every object will either reflect or absorb the individual rays of white light in different degrees, resulting in colour. White objects reflect back all the rays so they absorb no colour, while black objects absorb all the rays. Objects that appear green absorb all the rays except the green, which they reflect back, and so on with all the other colours. This seems confusing at first, but there is a very simple experiment that will demonstrate this more clearly.

As I have already said, light (and therefore colour) is electromagnetic radiation, which is a form of energy. All energies produce heat. As we know, each colour has its own wavelength, and when these are reflected from a surface they emit heat. If you put two tin plates out in the sun, one black and one white, and leave them both there for one hour, which one do you think will be hotter? Most of us know it will be the black plate, but you may not have known why until now. The reason is that the white plate has reflected all the rays back, and therefore not only has it absorbed no colour, but it has also absorbed none of the energy or heat contained within the colour. The black plate has absorbed all the rays, and thus all the energy and heat. Different objects appear as different colours because they will either reflect or absorb the individual rays of white light in different degrees, resulting in colour.

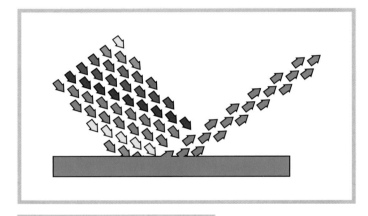

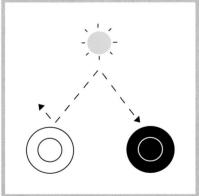

The diagram above shows how coloured objects reflect their own colour, and therefore, all of the energy (and heat) that is associated with that particular colour or wavelength.

The diagram on the left shows how white objects reflect all the rays contained in white light (and therefore the energy), while black objects absorb all the rays.

This explains how different objects appear as different colours, but we also need to look at how exactly we see colour. The lens of the eye views an object in much the same way as a camera does. The light reflected from the object enters the eye through the lens and an image is formed on the back wall of the eye, which is called the retina. The retina is covered with millions of nerve endings called rods which are stimulated by the light falling on them. The rods cannot register colour, they register only degrees of black and white, or what we call the 'tonal quality' of an object. In the centre of the back wall of the retina is a small depression, which is called the fovea. The fovea contains millions of nerve endings called cones, and these cones record colour. Both the rods and cones send these light stimuli to the brain, where they are transformed into an image of the object. So then, seeing is actually a function of the brain and not of the eye itself, which explains why some people who suffer brain damage, but whose eyes are functioning normally, suffer from blindness.

When we take a closer look at the plate experiment, it clearly illustrates how different objects reflect or absorb not only colour, but also the energy or heat which is connected with that colour. Anybody working with colour is aware that there are warm and cool colours, but you can clearly see that this is not just a label – certain colours really are warm and others are cool. If we take a look around, evidence of this is everywhere. In warm countries, the exteriors of houses are often painted white to reflect the sun, and the interiors will usually be decorated using cool, light colours. In colder climates, warmer colours are more popular in interiors, with more elaborate window treatments and soft furnishings to increase the feeling of warmth. Very few people are actually aware of the science of colour, yet they commonly choose colours that are right for their environment when they follow their own intuition. Up until fairly recently, theories about the different aspects of colour have been dismissed as 'new-age' thinking or 'off the wall', but now discoveries are being made which prove what many people have known all along – that colour is an energy, energy produces heat, and therefore colour affects temperature.

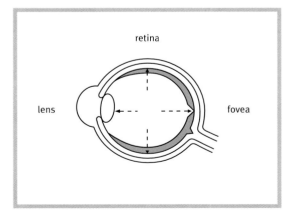

This diagram shows the retina of the eye and the fovea at the back, which are covered in rods and cones respectively to record tones and colour.

Scientific studies have shown that there are people so sensitive to colour that, even when blindfolded, they can distinguish colours with their fingertips. What's even more interesting is that this ability was not as exceptional as it seemed at first. Indeed, after only 20–30 minutes training, one out of six experimental subjects could recognise colour with their fingertips. At first, it seemed logical to assume that these individuals were extremely sensitive to heat and this was how they were able to differentiate between the individual colours, but now science is revealing that there is much more to it than this. In further studies, the same individuals were still able to distinguish colours accurately, even when the colours were put under glass, aluminium foil, or even brass or copper plates. The heat generated by the colour was obviously not a factor in this case, so there is obviously more to colour than just heat. Although this is still puzzling scientists as they haven't fully discovered how this works yet, they have recently understood how colour affects our moods and our emotions.

As each particular colour wavelength hits the cones in the eye (which are the colour receptors), they are converted into electrical impulses which pass to the brain, where they are converted into images. Eventually they reach the hypothalamus, an area of the brain, which governs the endocrine glands. The endocrine system in our bodies is responsible for producing and secreting our hormones. Each colour or wavelength focuses on a particular part of the body, evoking a specific physiological response, which in turn produces a psychological reaction. So then, colour is actually a sensation that our brain registers, and not a physical property of the object we are viewing. We have already established that 'seeing colour' is actually a function of the brain and not of the eyes, and this is why blind people are affected by colour in the same way that sighted people are.

This science is quite new, but it validates that not only does colour produce physical and emotional responses within us, but that individual colours are responsible for specific areas of our bodies. As we have seen in Chapter 1, this is something that has been widely accepted in the Eastern world and in the therapeutic use of colour for centuries. Now Western science is arriving at the same conclusions, even though we have approached the subject from an entirely different angle. Colour psychology studies the effects that individual colours have on people and the feelings and emotions that they create. This topic is obviously of paramount importance to the interior designer, who works so intimately with colour, and personally I find this a fascinating subject. We will be exploring it further in chapter 8 and looking at the implications for interior design. For the moment, let's take a closer look at the theory of colour.

Some people are so sensitive to colour that even blindfolded, they can correctly identify different colours.

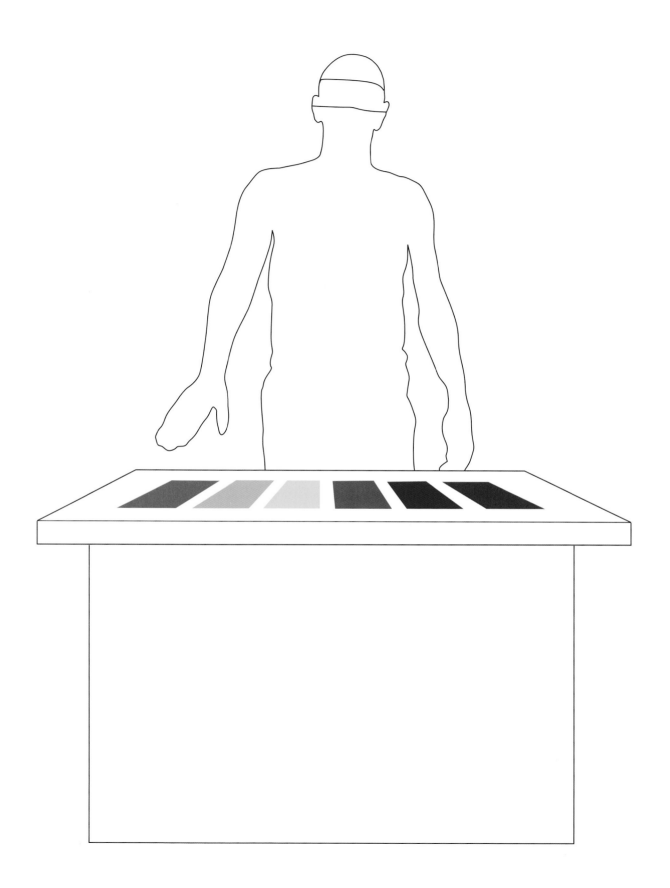

chapter **3**   colour theory

In this chapter we will demonstrate how the millions of colours that exist around us can all be created from the seven colours of the spectrum. The previous chapter clearly illustrated how colour is basically just shattered light, and that different objects appear as different colours according to the varying degrees that they absorb or reflect that light. A technical point that we need to clarify before going any further though, is the difference between coloured light and coloured pigment. In the theoretical study of colour, this is known as 'additive' and 'subtractive' colour.

Simply put, all of the objects that we see around us are given their colour by various pigments or dyes, and this is known technically as 'subtractive colour'. We will soon see how mixing certain colours together will result in an entirely new colour, and we will also explain the definition of primaries and secondaries, etc. However, you must take note that coloured light behaves slightly differently to coloured pigments. When coloured light is mixed together the primary colours are different and therefore they will be mixed differently. This type of colour is referred to as 'additive colour'. In everyday practice, mixing coloured light is not something that we will usually involve ourselves with, and this is the only place that we will refer to the distinction between additive and subtractive colour. In the study of interior design, all of the colour we deal with is pigment-based and therefore subtractive colour.

About 100 years after Newton discovered the spectrum, the German scientist Goethe gave us a very useful tool when he created the colour wheel. Goethe took the band of colours that make up the spectrum and, without changing the natural order, he joined the ends to form a circle, creating the first colour wheel. He made no changes to the colours or their order, except for replacing indigo and violet with the single colour purple. This seemed more sensible as they were so closely related, and the end result was a colour wheel divided into six equal parts.

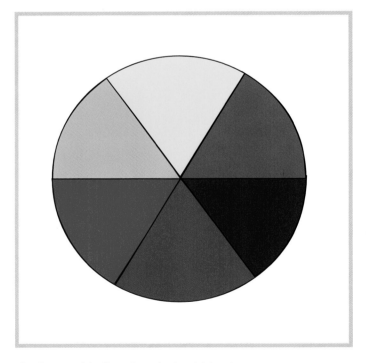

Goethe created the first colour wheel containing six segments, which clearly shows the relationship between primary and secondary colours.

Once he had constructed the colour wheel, Goethe noticed something quite exciting; the colours that can be mixed fell between colours that cannot be mixed. For instance, red, yellow and blue are the three colours that contain no trace of any other colour and cannot be mixed from another colour. However, green can be mixed from yellow and blue, which lie on either side of green on the colour wheel. Likewise, orange can be mixed from red and yellow, and purple can be mixed from red and blue. Goethe called the colours that cannot be mixed primary colours, and the other three he called secondaries. The colour wheel can be extended further by continuing to mix colours in this way, introducing tertiary colours and so on. (In Chapter 5 we will take a closer look at this and see how Albert Munsell created a wheel with 100 segments, indicating very gradual changes from one colour to the next.)

Through his studies, Goethe illustrated how one colour gradually changes into another, and he gave us a very valuable tool – the colour wheel. Many designers and artists today still use a colour wheel to help them plan colour schemes and help them mix colour successfully, and they can be easily purchased at good art shops. Most of the colour wheels that you will come across usually consist of 12 segments, containing primaries, secondaries and tertiaries. The diagram illustrates how this looks.

When constructing a colour wheel (whether it has six or 100 segments), the same natural order is always observed. Because yellow is the lightest colour, it is usually placed at the top of the wheel. Purple, being the darkest colour, is placed at the bottom. If we draw a line vertically through the centre of the colour wheel, all the colours to the left of this line are warm, whereas all the colours to the right are cool. We will examine the relationship between warm and cool colours in later chapters, but we should also note here that all of the colour wheel hues are strong, vivid colours. Although we use and experience these colours in everyday life, soft pastels and muted, dusky colours are more common. So then, where do they all come from and how can we create them – if all colours are mixed from the hues of the colour wheel?

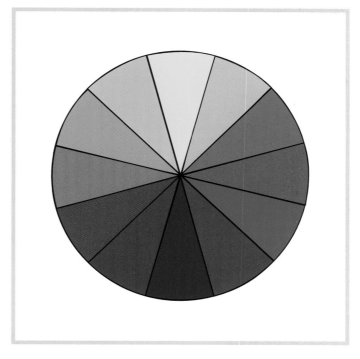

The 12-segment colour wheel includes tertiaries. Always remember to place yellow at the top of the wheel.

So far we have not talked about black and white as colours. Strictly speaking they are not considered colours, because they are not represented on the colour wheel, but black and white can be added to the pure hues of the colour wheel to create different tones of colour, and to sometimes change the colour completely. Neutral greys, which are a combination of black and white, can also be added to these colours or used on their own. Once you add black and white to the pure hues of the colour wheel, by experimenting with different quantities, the possibilities seem endless and millions of colours can be achieved. To make life a little easier and avoid confusion in our language, let's look at a few definitions before we go any further.

Achromatic colours Although we describe these as achromatic colours, achromatic colour consists of only black and white, and mixtures of black and white which are greys.

Chromatic colours All other colours (i.e. red in its pure form or with white added to form pink) are known as chromatic colours. It is important to understand this definition and to know the difference between the two.

Hues The pure colours taken from the colour wheel.

Primary colour A primary colour is one that cannot be mixed from any combination of other colours. It contains no trace whatsoever of any other colour, and will appear to be visibly pure in itself. There are only three primary colours – red, yellow and blue.

Secondary colours These are created when primary colours are mixed, and the secondary colours are: green, purple and orange.

Tints These are colours to which white has been added, no matter how small the quantity. The colour will appear lighter in tone than the original.

Shades These are colours to which black has been added. Generally these appear as more muted tones.

Pastel colours These are pure colours to which white and black have been added in equal quantities. This produces a grey, softer colour, which is a popular choice in decorating.

Pastel tints These are composed by adding equal amounts of black and white to create a pastel colour. Then extra white is added to make a pastel tint.

Pastel shades Likewise, pastel shades have more black than white in their mix.

Tone This refers to the lightness or darkness of a colour.

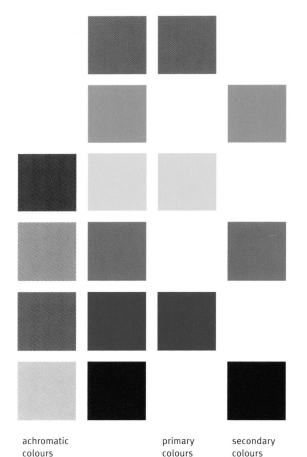

achromatic colours

primary colours

secondary colours

Discordant colour

There are times when colour seems out of harmony
with the natural order and this is known as discordant
colour. In a discordant colour wheel, yellow becomes the
darkest colour, and purple becomes the lightest. The
term is not used very often, and discordant colours are
usually perceived as quite unpleasant. Like all colours
though, they have their uses, and careful planning can
bring out the best in any colour scheme if you ever find
yourself working with them. Though you may not want
to deliberately create a discordant colour scheme
yourself, knowledge of this may also help you to
understand why some schemes aren't working.

By now you should clearly see how combining various
hues together with various quantities of black and white
will enable you to create literally millions of different
colours. In Chapter 5, we will examine this topic in even
more detail, and this will help us to understand the
individual components that make up each colour, and
how any colour can be reproduced with consistent
quality. Before we go into technicalities again though,
let's have a bit of fun and take a look at some of the
contrasts that can be created using the colour wheel
and how we can apply this to create stunning interiors.

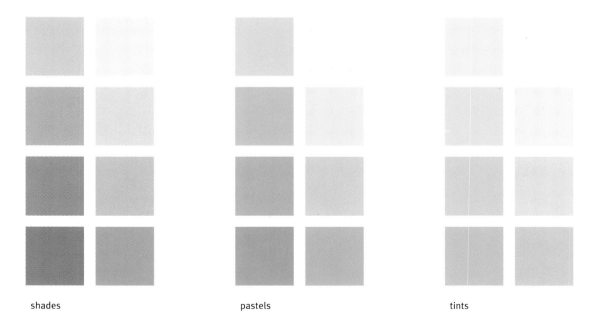

shades   pastels   tints

creating harmonious colour schemes

chapter **4**

When singers match their voices and sing in unison, although each individual sings in his or her own key, together they harmonise, creating a pleasing sound for us to hear. This is harmony in song, and colour harmony works in a very similar way. To create a colour scheme that is visually pleasing, you have to learn how to choose colours that work together harmoniously, in the same way as musical notes. And, just as there is a huge variety in musical styles, there is an equally diverse range of colour combinations that suits all our personal tastes.

Whatever your individual preferences, you should be able to look at any colour scheme and instantly tell if it is in harmony or not. Being able to appreciate the elements of a successful decor scheme will help you to expand your personal preferences, and you will probably find that your tastes will change, allowing you to choose from a wider variety of decorating styles to express yourself. It will also allow you to create successful schemes for other people, even if the style is not to your own taste, and this is absolutely essential for professional designers. With music, we may prefer to listen to pop or a classical piece, but when we listen to a country and western song, we can still tell if the singers are in harmony or if they are singing flat notes. So what is the secret to creating a harmonious colour scheme?

Firstly, there is no such thing as a bad colour, only bad use of colour. An individual colour that might look very strong or gaudy when standing on its own, can be 'transformed' if it is accompanied by other harmonious colours which either blend subtly, or highlight and complement it. By choosing colours that harmonise in this way, the whole appearance of a colour will change before your eyes. The way that colours interact with each other in this manner is known technically as 'simultaneous contrast' and we will look at this in more detail in Chapter 6. In this chapter we are going to look at some of the guidelines that designers and artists have used for many years and see how you can use the colour wheel to select colours that will always work together successfully, and so create your own harmonious schemes. This will provide you with a very useful reference tool when you are looking for inspiration, or when you have to work with existing colours that might seem difficult at first.

Before we go any further, it is important to remember that achieving the right colour balance is the base for any successful scheme, and it is essential that you take time at the planning stage to match colour swatches and samples, checking for compatibility. An interior may make use of luxurious marbles and expensive silk fabrics, but if the colours are clashing, the overall effect could be cheap and garish. When you are using several colours in the same scheme, there needs to be some degree of unity throughout the scheme for it to be successful. Roughly translated, this means if you use a pastel green, make sure the other colours are pastels too, so that the tones are harmonious, no matter which type of contrast you select. Without contrast, any scheme will be bland and uninteresting, but the type of contrast you decide to use will depend on individual tastes or the mood you are trying to create. Contrasts can be subtle or strong, so let's take a look at some.

These pictures illustrate the effect of simultaneous contrast, and how the same colour orange can create a completely different effect depending on the surrounding colours and quantities.

Monochromatic contrast

As the name suggests, a monochromatic colour scheme is based on one colour and uses different tones of that colour to create contrast. Ideally the tonal mix should include light, medium and dark tones to create the right balance, and it is a scheme that requires careful attention so that it doesn't become too boring. In this type of scheme the contrast between the various tones generally creates a very subtle design, so creating visual interest by using contrasting textures, patterns and lines can be very important. Another way to relieve monotony is with the use of an accent colour that contrasts with the main colour. Of course neutral colours can be mixed with any colour scheme and achromatic colours are also considered neutral for these purposes.

A monochromatic scheme in which the same hue is used in the same, consistent intensity is sometimes referred to as a monotone scheme. An all-white scheme, for instance (as is popular in the minimalist style), would be seen as a monotone version of a monochromatic scheme. All-cream schemes tend to be very popular with designers, and they do have a timeless appeal. However, in this type of scheme texture and form are an absolute necessity to prevent the end result looking dull and lifeless. Even the folds in the fabric of the curtains for instance, will add visual relief through the shadows and highlights created.

Analogous (or harmonious) schemes

Hues that are close together on the colour wheel seem closely related and are therefore visually harmonious. Analogous schemes can be created by using as few as two colours lying next to each other on the wheel, or as many as four colours. This is a very popular choice for colour schemes, and analogous colours usually create a very calm, soothing contrast, which is generally subtle.

Many people enjoy strong colours but don't necessarily like the effect of combining too many different hues, and this is one reason why analogous schemes have an enduring popularity. An analogous colour scheme allows the use of strong colours, but because the variation between the hues is less intense, this seems to balance the visual impact. On those occasions when there is a need for more visual impact, then an analogous scheme can be given more life by using an accent hue from the opposite side of the colour wheel. Even a small accessory item in an accent colour can change the feel of the room quite radically, and it is something that can be temporarily added to suit the mood.

Triadic contrast

Choosing three colours from the colour wheel that are at equal distances from each other will create a triadic colour scheme. When used in their pure hue, this makes for quite a strong contrast, the greatest being that between the three primary colours – red, yellow and blue. As we move through the colour wheel to the secondary and tertiary colours, the contrast will still be quite strong, but it decreases the further we go. You could be forgiven for thinking that this kind of contrast would have limited use in interior design, but it is far more widespread than most people imagine. The most obvious use for strong primary colours is in children's rooms. Children adore these colours from a very early age and this is the reason why so many toys and children's clothes are produced in them. The thought of painting nursery walls in red, blue and yellow might seem a little overwhelming, so very often whites and creams are used as a background to the stronger hues and provide the eyes with visual relief. An attractive look can be achieved by painting items of furniture and adding colourful pictures and accessories. There are many fabrics and wallpapers produced specifically for children's tastes, and these can create fun, lively rooms, but don't forget to consider the colour psychology as well, so that you don't encourage hyperactivity.

For the adult population, strong chromatic contrasts can still produce stunning results if they are carefully used. If overdone this type of palette could become irritating and stressful, but for the most part, choosing accessories in triadic colours can help to bring a room to life. A triad contrast is playful and lively, and can be quite rich, depending on the style of the interior you are looking for. Thoughtful planning can result in a truly unique and fun effect.

Complementary contrast

As the name implies, complementary contrast is
between two colours which naturally complement each
other and are directly opposite each other on the colour
wheel. They will usually be very strong contrasts as they
will be opposite in both hue and colour temperature,
and these colours will always intensify each other. For
instance, red will make green look greener, and vice
versa. At the same time, each colour will provide visual
relief from its complementary, and it is always a good
idea to use some element of complementary colour
within a scheme, particularly when working with strong
hues. These types of contrasts create a strong impact
when colours are used in their pure form, but the
intensity is lessened when, for instance, pastels
are used.

Split complementary contrast

This is a variation on a complementary contrast, where
a hue from one side of the colour wheel is used with the
two hues that lie on either side of its complementary
colour. Schemes based on split complementary colours
allow a little more flexibility than complementary
contrasts, but the same rules generally apply.

Double complementary contrast

Still another variation, this makes use of two adjacent
hues on the colour wheel, and their complementary
colours. Basically this results in a colour scheme that
makes use of two sets of analogous colours. A scheme
based on this type of contrast would be quite active,
and would generally need careful handling if it was not
to look too disjointed or random. However, if the tones
are carefully balanced, an attractive scheme can be
created as shown in the illustration.

Tetrad

This type of colour scheme uses four hues that are
spaced equally around the colour wheel, resulting in a
scheme that is composed of two sets of
complementaries. A tetrad colour scheme uses hues
from each part of the colour wheel and is quite active in
its effect. There is a danger of it becoming over-varied or
chaotic, so care must be taken to avoid confusion of
colour. It is quite a difficult colour relationship to use
successfully, and one hue is usually dominant. Although
it can be useful, it is generally a difficult choice of
contrast to work with.

So far we have not looked at achromatics or neutral
tones, neither of which are represented on the colour
wheel. Technically they are termed 'non-colours', but
they can be used to create very successful decor
schemes and they remain a popular choice for many
interior designers.

Achromatic contrast

Achromatic contrast is the difference between black
and white or between mixes of the two, which are greys.
The most noticeable contrast is obviously that between
black and white, and this colour combination can be
used in an interior to achieve very dramatic results.
Although most people tend to think of sleek, modern
styles when we talk about black and white schemes, it
is in fact a very classical choice, which continues to
have timeless appeal. In recent years particularly, a
renewed popularity in architectural prints and
botanical drawings has inspired many new fabric
and wallpaper collections.

Equally, black and white can be used to create
wonderful contemporary designs and it remains a
popular choice for many designers. An eye for the right
details in materials and accessories can bring warmth
and character to this colour scheme, but it requires
careful handling if it is not to become stark and severe.
With no other colours to distract the eye, these
schemes ruthlessly draw attention to detail, so
furnishings and accessories must be carefully selected.
Generally a lot of thought must be given to the form and
line of each item chosen.

The main point to consider when choosing an
achromatic scheme is that it needs to be carried out
with consistency and conviction to be effective. With no
other colours to distract the eye, each detail becomes
increasingly important. On a day-to-day basis it can be
difficult to live with, as it requires extreme tidiness to
look good. For this reason black and white schemes
work well in kitchens and bathrooms, where they can
create an atmosphere of efficiency and cleanliness.

Accent colours

A good idea to help relieve the potential starkness of an
achromatic scheme is to introduce at least one accent
colour to provide visual relief. This can be done by
including natural materials such as rich wooden
furniture or natural limestone flooring, or indeed by
using colourful accessories. A few bursts of strong, bold
colour, or a subtle combination of soft pastels can be
excellent choices when used thoughtfully. By simply
changing the accent colours of cushions, flowers and
other small accessories, for instance, a completely new
look can be achieved very easily. This can be adapted
to suit different occasions or seasons, or even your
own moods.

Neutral schemes

In theory, the only true neutral colours are the achromatics that we have just looked at, but of course in the real decorating world, 'neutrals' can be the designer's best friend. Beiges, browns, creams and stone colours all fall into this category, and most decorating schemes will make use of neutrals as a background for some of the stronger colour contrasts. Using neutrals in this way can provide visual relief and at the same time, an unobtrusive background that will highlight the main colours. Skilfully used, they can either tone down or bring into focus bold colours in a scheme, and they can help to unify a design that incorporates several colours, particularly when they are used on large areas such as flooring.

Neutral colours can be compared with those that are found in the earth, and as such, are commonly used to create very natural interiors, that are both calming and restful. This is one of the reasons why they are so popular. The other reason is that even most novice decorators feel capable of managing a neutral scheme successfully, and they consider them a safe bet.

While this is often true, like any monochromatic scheme, they need careful handling if they are not to become dull and boring. The trick again is to use contrasting textures and patterns. Natural forms and shapes also provide an interesting focal point for the eyes.

Although any colour scheme can make use of neutrals, care must be taken to match samples and colour swatches as normal. Not all neutrals will have the same base colour, and when they are examined closely, some beiges, for instance, might be based on a reddish hue, whereas others might have a yellow base. It is important to choose a neutral with a base colour that is complementary to the rest of the scheme.

On those rare occasions when you have matched your samples and planned properly, yet the end result is still not working, it could be the tonal mix that is wrong. As we have said already, when you are working with a number of colours it is important to get the balance of tones right between them, but that's not always as easy as it sounds. In the next chapter we will take a more detailed look at tone and the other dimensions that make up individual colours. We will literally pick colours apart piece by piece, so you will understand exactly what it is you are dealing with.

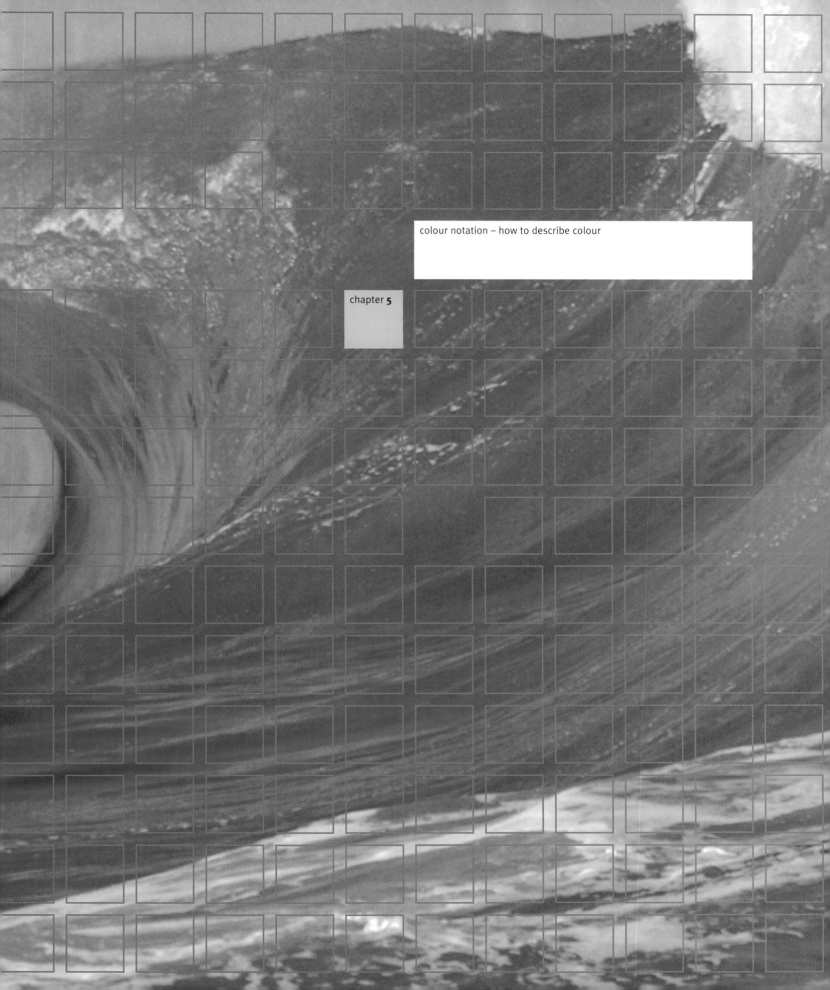

colour notation – how to describe colour

chapter **5**

Greens

Take a look at the three different types of green below.
Now taking each one in turn, try to describe each colour
as accurately as you can. You must describe each colour
individually, without referring to any of the others. For
instance, you cannot say that 'B' is darker than 'A', or 'C'
is brighter than 'B' etc. Take a minute now to do this.

It's more difficult than it seems, isn't it?

A

B

C

One reason that it is so hard to describe colours is that
there are only 11 words in the English language that are
used solely to describe colour. The rest of the words that
we use on a day-to-day basis are borrowed from nature.
For example, cream, cornflower blue, forest green, etc.

This is one of the reasons it was considered very
important to create a system of colour notation that
would a) accurately describe colours, and b) be so
precise that this would allow the same colours to be
reproduced anywhere in the world.

white

/9

/8

/7

/6

/5

/4

/3

value ▶

/2   /2   /4   /6   /8   /10   /12

/1   chroma ▶

black

Although a number of colour systems have been developed throughout the years, the most widely used is the Munsell system, and this is favoured by companies throughout the world that require precise methods of reproducing colour. The system is quite technical, and you will rarely (if ever) need to examine colours to this degree of accuracy. However, by understanding the way the Munsell system works, you will have a much greater understanding of colour and you will be able to describe colour more accurately to others.

Albert Munsell first created and published his colour notation system in 1915. When he died in 1918, the Munsell Colour Company was formed to carry on his work, and they are still in operation today. As well as producing various student chart sets and colour slides, the Munsell Colour Company also produce colour standards which are widely used by geologists, archeologists, and biologists, etc. to determine such things as nutrient deficiency in plants and soil. They even produce a colour chart that is used by anthropologists to classify skin, hair and eye colours. The list of products could continue further, but these examples are sufficient to illustrate the extent and efficiency to which the Munsell Colour Company has developed their system. So how does the Munsell system of colour notation apply to interior design?

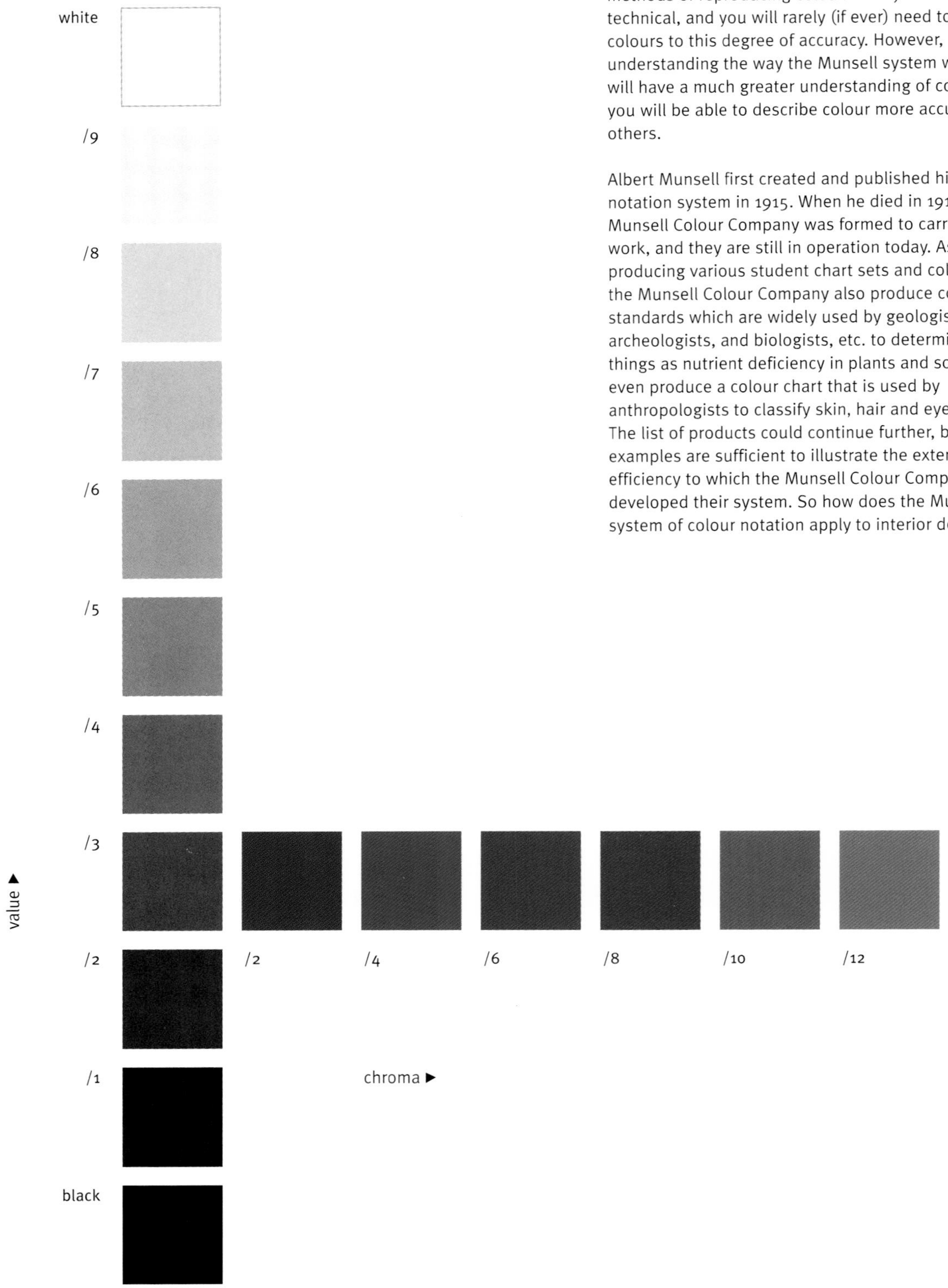

Albert Munsell identified that every colour consists of three dimensions or variables. In order for a colour to be described accurately, each of these dimensions must be represented in a formula. The dimensions of colour are:

1 *Hue*: This is the quality that distinguishes one colour family from another. For instance red or green, etc.

2 *Value*: This determines the lightness or darkness of a colour, otherwise known as the tone.

3 *Chroma*: This describes the strength or purity of a colour. For instance a bright, pure blue or a dull, grey blue.

Let's take a look at these in more detail.

hue

value

chroma

Hue

As we have already said, the hue is the quality that
distinguishes one colour from another, and the first
reference in a Munsell colour code indicates which hue
the colour we are looking at is based on.

The Munsell system can be a little confusing, because
first off, it is based on a colour wheel that uses five
principle hues, rather than the three primary hues that
we are already familiar with from Goethe's colour wheel.

The five principal hues used are red, yellow, green, blue
and purple. In between each of these hues lie five
intermediary hues. The entire Munsell system is based
on this ten-hue colour circle.

We have already seen how mixing primary colours
produces secondaries, and mixing secondaries produces
tertiaries. Of course this can be continued to produce
even more intermediary colours, so that we end up with
a large colour wheel that registers extremely gradual
changes from one colour to the next. Munsell applied
this method to his ten-segment colour wheel, gradually
combining hues more and more until he ended up with a
colour wheel that has 100 segments. Each of these
divisions has to be labelled, and in order to keep things
as simple as possible, Munsell numbered each hue
segment from one to ten.

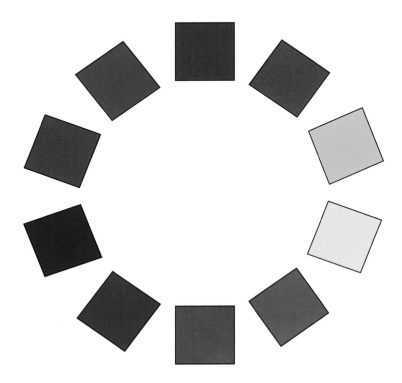

Munsell's ten-segment colour wheel showing
ten hues at strong chroma.

For instance, the ten red divisions would be numbered 1R, 2R, 3R etc. through to 10R. After 10R, the divisions of the next colour (yellow-red) take over, starting at 1YR, 2YR and so on through to 10YR. The hue that lies at number five is always a pure hue and will show no trace of the other colours. This results in a colour wheel that has 100 hue segments, each with their own reference.

A Munsell colour reference contains the information necessary to reproduce a colour exactly, and the hue is always the first element to be identified. We will look at how exactly this all works together when we have analysed all three elements. The next element to consider is the value.

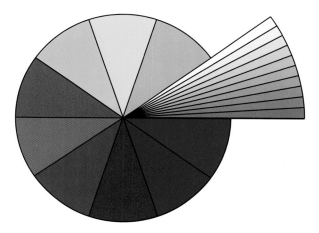

The ten-segment colour wheel.

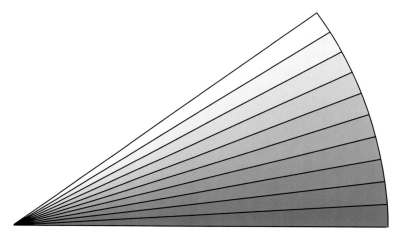

A section of the 100-segment colour wheel.

Value

This quality enables us to distinguish a light colour from
a dark colour. As the first reference only tells us about
the hue, so the value reference will only tell us about
the lightness or darkness of the colour. (In everyday
speech, we usually refer to this as the tone.) To indicate
value, Munsell divided the difference between black and
white into nine visually equal steps of grey, and
numbered them one to nine (see page 58). These greys
are referred to as neutral greys as they are made from
black and white and are entirely achromatic. Black was
numbered zero and white ten. The tone of a colour is
checked against this scale, and given a value number
accordingly. A low value would indicate a dark colour
(such as a shade), while a high value (eight for instance)
would indicate a light colour such as a tint.

Whichever colour is to be described, it will be held up
against this scale to see how light or dark it is and given
a number accordingly. In everyday practice, it is
sometimes quite hard to determine the value or tone of
a colour, as we are often distracted by the hue. If you
want to practice looking purely at the value, hold the
colour at arm's length and then squint your eyes while
looking at it. This will blur the hue slightly and the value
will be more apparent.

Another exercise you can try is to take a swatch card of
paint samples and photocopy it on a standard black and
white photocopier. The photocopy will obviously have
no colour on it and will show only the tones. By
comparing the original paint swatch with the copy, you
will become more familiar with assessing the tone of
any colour.

Back to the Munsell reference, and the final element
referred to which is the chroma.

Chroma

The chroma reference number tells us how saturated a
colour is – whether the colour is pure and intense, or
grey and without much colour. In the Munsell system,
the chroma reference radiates outwards from the neutral
grey scale, again in visually equal steps. Each step is
numbered in multiples of two, and continues to a
maximum of usually 14 or 16 steps (see page 58).

value   chroma

This is the part of the system that usually causes the most confusion, so take time to digest this information slowly. I find the easiest way to explain this is to work backwards.

Visualise for a moment the value scale and imagine that each value is a pot of grey paint. Taking the value of number eight, let's imagine that there is a whole row of paint pots in a line with the same value. In this example, we are looking at a colour that is based on a red hue, so we will begin by adding two drops of red paint into the first grey pot at value number eight. By doing so, we have changed the colour, even if it is only slight. In reality, you probably wouldn't even notice the difference too much, as this is only enough chroma to change the undertone. The resulting colour is a high value, based on a red hue, but there is a low level of chroma – which is intensity of colour. To the next pot we will add four drops of red paint. The resulting colour is stronger than the previous one, there is obviously a higher level of chroma.

Not all colours reach their maximum chroma at the same level of steps. To explain, all pure hues are very strong. By adding red to a number eight grey, it will not take very many steps for the colour to reach maximum depth as we are looking at a light tone. If we continue to add more drops of red past the number of 12 for instance, the resulting colour will not only be stronger in chroma, but will also be a darker colour – resulting in a higher value. For this reason, the Munsell system is not a neat, uniform shape. However, this allows for the most flexibility and for newly discovered colours to continue to be added into the system without rearranging the entire structure.

So then, the Munsell system describes all colours in the same way. First of all, there is a reference to the base hue. After a space, the next number refers to the value scale, and an oblique stroke separates this from the last reference number which relates to the chroma level. This looks like the following:

5BG 3/12: This would refer to a colour that is based on a pure blue-green. It has a low value of three, so it would be quite dark in tone, but the high chroma value of 12 would indicate that it is quite an intense colour.
10RP 8/4: This would refer to a colour that is based on red-purple, that has far more purple than red present in the mix. The high value of eight would indicate that it is quite light in tone, with a low chroma content. This would probably be a pink colour that looks slightly more blue than red.

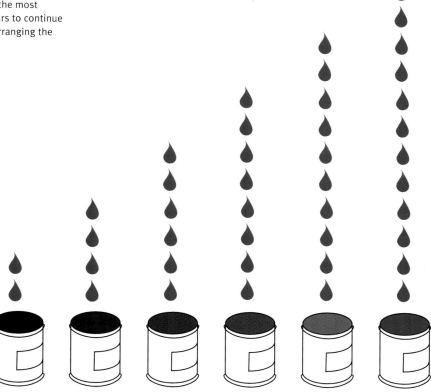

The modified system of notation

From a scientific point of view, the Munsell system of notation is extremely accurate in its description of colours and it is the best choice when complete precision is required. Paint manufacturers all over the world use this system, so that the same colours can be consistently produced. However, this method of describing colour is not really practical for general use on a day-to-day basis – but we can modify it.

Firstly, let's go back to our own 12-segment colour wheel, consisting of primaries, secondaries and tertiaries. We already know that these 12 colours provide the base for all other colours. In our modified approach, colour is still described in the three dimensions of hue, value and chroma. But as follows;

Hue: We describe colour according to its position on the colour wheel. If a 12-segment colour wheel is used, then tertiary hues will be described as blue-green, yellow-orange etc.

Value or tone: As we have already said, in everyday speech it is more common for us to refer to the tone of a colour, rather than the value. As this clearly refers to the lightness or darkness of a colour, it makes sense to keep language simple and refer to each colour as such. By referring to a colour as light, medium or dark, it is fairly easy to get a visual image of where on the scale this colour would be regarding tone. This can be narrowed down even more by describing a colour as medium, or light-toned, etc.

Chroma or saturation: As we know, this refers to the purity or intensity of a colour, and so tells us whether a colour is 'bright' and intense or 'dull'. A 'pale' colour suggests a light value at low saturation, while 'deep' indicates a darker value at high saturation.

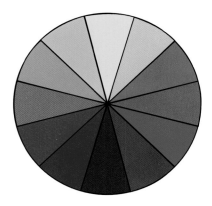

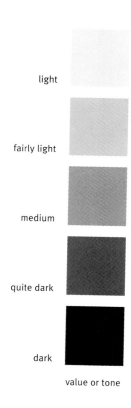

light

fairly light

medium

quite dark

dark

value or tone

The value in studying the Munsell system comes from the practical way in which it organises the variables or dimensions of colour. Not only does this give us a much deeper awareness of colour, but it also allows us to choose and develop colour schemes in an orderly and logical way, and to communicate our choices to others. For the most part in interior design, we usually select and communicate colours to each other through samples rather than colour systems. But choosing colour is mainly intuitive and without this understanding it can be quite difficult to explain to clients why a suggested scheme will work. When they are paying large amounts of money, very few clients will proceed with a daring scheme based purely on the designer's gut instinct. This modified system of colour notation helps designers to explain precisely why the scheme they have selected will work, and it instils confidence in the clients' decision to employ you in the first place.

While this modified version of colour notation or description is not nearly as precise as Munsell's system, it will serve us well in everyday use and help us to choose and describe colour with confidence. To demonstrate, while the Munsell notation 7YR 8/6 does not readily bring a colour to mind, the description of 'a yellow-red that has a light tone and is quite bright' should enable you to visualise the colour being described. Now go back to the three different greens again (see page 56), and using this new knowledge, try once more to describe each colour individually.

It would probably be fair to say that 'A' is a yellow-green hue that has a medium tone and is quite intense in colour. 'B' is based on a blue-green hue. It has a light tone, but there is not much intensity of colour and it is quite dull and greyed. 'C' is based on a pure green hue. It is quite dark in tone and has intense colour.

Whether or not you agree precisely with my description is not very important, as we all perceive colours differently. The whole point of this exercise is that you should now have the knowledge and the vocabulary to describe colours more accurately and confidently. And by understanding how these colours work, you will be able to make more informed choices. By looking at colours closely we can describe more accurately the elements, and so the colours chosen. Remember, though, colour is a visual thing, and there is no substitute for a sample.

pale colour

quite bright

bright

quite strong

strong colour

modified scale of chroma

Other methods of mixing colour

It should be said that there are other ways of mixing colour, and if any of you are familiar with art techniques you will know that different hues can be combined in a number of ways to match up with existing colours. But there is a drawback to mixing colours in this was. For an artist to mix colours to be used in a painting like this, there won't be a problem. But if you mix paint colours like this for use in decorating, the mixture of hues creates an undertone, and this may knock your entire scheme out of balance. Let me tell you about a problem I once had with a painter that worked for me.

I specified the paints that I wanted used on a particular job and gave the painter a list of product codes and directions. I had chosen paint from a brand that I work with all the time and am extremely familiar with, and as always, I selected my paint colour from a large swatch card, so that all the variations of the colour could be seen. The particular paint that I favoured was quite expensive, and unbeknownst to me, the painter was trying to make some extra money on the side by replacing my paint with a cheap, inferior paint that was mixed to match the colour swatch. Unfortunately, the method of paint mixing was quite different from Munsell's method, and the base hue was not the same. When the paint was applied (to the ceiling in this case), it clashed terribly with the walls, and threw the entire decor off balance.

By holding the small swatch up to the ceiling, it was impossible to tell the difference between the two colours, and I thought I had made a mistake. The painter assured me that he had used the paint I had specified, and I had obviously made an error of judgement, so I chose another colour and asked him to repaint the ceiling. Again, the painter replaced my suggestion with a cheaper paint, and once more the colour clashed. At this point I knew something was up – I really didn't think I could have been so wrong in my judgement twice. I suspected what had happened, but again the painter denied this. Over the weekend, I went myself and purchased the original paint colour that I had specified and had somebody else re-paint the ceiling. The colour was perfect, and the room pulled together instantly.

The reason the cheaper paint didn't work had nothing to do with the price of the paint. The problem is that very few people working in the decorating industry understand the theory and science of colour, and many of them go about their own methods of mixing colours, particularly when they are using very small quantities. What happened in this case is that the base hue was different – indeed, the paint he used could have had several hues combined – and although it was impossible to tell the difference from the small swatch, the undertone showed through when it was painted on a large area.

When choosing paint colours, the easiest way to avoid this mistake is to always select a colour from the full sample card, showing the different levels of saturation from pale to dark. By looking at how the colour deepens further along the card, this helps to identify the hue more accurately and so ensure that it is complementary to the rest of the scheme.

Selecting paint colours from the full
sample card helps to identify the hue
more accurately and ensure that it is
complementary to the rest of the scheme.

Broken colour techniques

Another time when it is very important to look more deeply at colour is if you are planning to use one of the decorative paint finishes where colour is literally 'broken'. When this happens, the colour is altered quite dramatically sometimes. Once again, looking at the large swatch card should give you some idea as to how the colour will look when it starts to break up. For instance, if I want to create a terracotta colourwash I would look through the two swatch cards shown here. Sample card A shows the colour gradually fading into a light peach, and if I choose this brown for my colourwash, the result may be quite peachy. Sample card B shows the colour gradually changing into a light tan, but this is much closer to the type of colour that I want, so this would be my choice.

A word of warning, though: any time you are working with decorative paint effects, always have a sample done first before applying it to the walls. This is the one instance where the colour can alter quite a bit, and choosing paint this way will certainly help you to narrow down your paint choices, but it is no substitute for a sample.

The topic of colour systems and colour notation is by far the most complex when it comes to explaining colour theory, and when I lecture on this subject, most of my students struggle with this for a while before they understand it fully. So if it takes a little while to sink in, take your time and don't worry about it. It will suddenly all make sense to you, and it provides you with a most valuable tool.

card A   card B

chapter **6**

colour characteristics – real colour magic

In the chapter on colour theory, we already looked at the way different types of contrast (such as analogous, complementary, etc.) can be used to form the basis for a colour scheme. In this section we are going to look at the way individual colours interact with each other and how we can use colour to create illusions in decorating. All of this information applies to what you have already learnt about colour.

Simultaneous contrast, or colour interaction is the most important form of contrast for you to consider when decorating, and it is essential that you should familiarise yourself with how this works. Simply put:

Simultaneous contrast is the apparent ability of a colour to change its appearance when it is placed next to, or is completely surrounded by another colour.

This applies to achromatic and chromatic colours. If we take a square of medium grey colour, and surround it with white, the grey colour will appear dark by comparison with the white. If we take exactly the same square and place it on a black background, the grey will appear lighter by comparison with its darker surroundings. In the example shown, the exact same shade of grey is used on both squares.

Looking at a larger square of plain grey creates a different effect again. Obviously there is no surrounding colour to provide a contrast, so the grey seems more solid and intense.

The important point is that, although the same colour has been used in all of these examples, it appears different because it has been affected by the surrounding colour. Of course, this interaction between the various tones applies to all colours, so let's look at some more examples.

In the illustration on the right, a purple square is placed on a white and then a black background. Notice the same effect: how it appears darker on the white background than on the black. If we use two coloured backgrounds as shown, the effect is still the same: on the green background the purple appears darker, while on the brown it appears lighter.

Take note that it is not just the tone of the colour that is affected – the actual intensity of the colour can appear to be brighter or duller, depending on its surrounding colour. The size of the squares in relation to each other is also a very relevant factor. For instance, let's reverse these colours and view a large purple square with smaller squares of the other colours, and observe the difference in how they look.

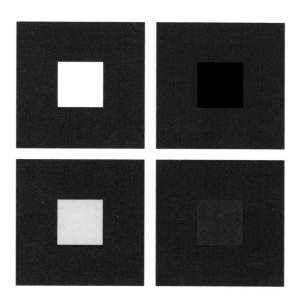

At this point you may be wondering where exactly we are going with this, and let's face it, looking at small coloured squares may not excite you very much, but when this is applied to interior design it can produce stunning results. Before we see exactly how to apply this, there are two main points to take note of: firstly, any colour can appear pleasing or not to the eye, depending on the other colours that are used with it. And secondly, the overall size of a colour area also seems to be an important factor in the way the colour is perceived. Simply put, smaller samples can appear lighter, darker, or more or less intense than when they are applied to a large surface, and without practice, it can be hard to visualise a whole room from a small paint sample. Indeed, the colour may look completely different than you originally intended when it is applied to a large area, as the following examples will show.

Stronger colours can appear too much on large areas, but when used in smaller quantities or with splashes of colour here and there, the results can be more successful. A very popular trick is to use a colour on only one or two walls so that the intensity is lessened, yet you still have the effect of using a vibrant hue.

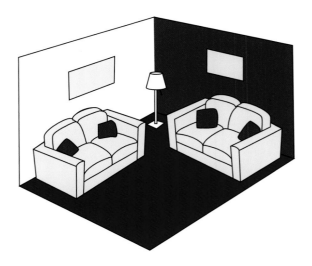

The effect of simultaneous contrast, and the way that colours interact with each other is so important to remember when planning your schemes, and particularly as your schemes are in the process of being executed. Very often, especially when working with strong colours, panic can set in when the colour is first applied to the wall. When nothing else is in the room to complement and tone down the colours, any single colour can appear overwhelming. Clients have often shown pure terror at this stage in the decorating, yet once I have taken the time to plan the scheme properly, I can assure them with confidence to trust me. I know that once all the other elements have gone into the room, the effect will be what I set out to achieve in the first place. So always bear this in mind.

Complementary colours

As we have already seen in Chapter 4, complementary colours are pairs of colours that are directly opposite each other on the colour wheel. We have already seen how using complementary colours in a decorating scheme makes for quite a strong contrast, and that these colours will always intensify each other and will generally be pleasing to the eye. However, there is another aspect to them. By placing a square of neutral grey on a strong green background, and then placing the same grey on a strong red background, see if you can observe the following:

On the green background, the grey square appears to take on a slightly reddish hue. While on the red background, the opposite occurs and the grey square appears to take on a slightly greenish hue. The effect is slight, but you should see it if you look carefully.

Quite extensive studies have been carried out in this area, and it has been shown that when we are presented with a strong colour, our eyes tire of the strain, and the brain naturally produces the complementary colour to modify the effect and balance this out. This can be difficult to see on such a small example, so do the following exercise:

Stare at the red circle on the right for about 60 seconds, focusing solely on the circle. When the minute is up, transfer your eyes to a plain white surface and keep staring at the surface for a further 60 seconds. Do this now before reading any more.

You should have seen an after-image on the white surface of a green circle – the complementary colour of red. If you did this experiment with a blue circle or indeed any other colour, you would see its complementary colour as an after-image. This should illustrate how placing two complementary colours together in a scheme, even though this makes for a strong contrast, will add balance and modify the effect of using such strong colours. Because of this, when you are working with strong colours it can be a good idea to try to incorporate the complementary colour into the scheme, even if it is just a minor accent colour.

Warm and cool colours

As we have already described in Chapter 2, colour and temperature have a very real relationship, and certain colours are known as warm, while others are known as cool. The way to determine which is which, is to draw a vertical line directly through the colour wheel dividing it into two equal halves. The hues to the left of this line, yellow-orange, orange, red-orange, red and red-purple are known as the warm colours. The remaining colours on the right of this line, yellow-green, green, blue-green, blue and blue-purple are known as cool colours. Note that the dividing line cuts through yellow and purple. Yellow is viewed by most people as a warm colour, but if it has any trace of green whatsoever, it may feel cool. For the same reason, purple can be viewed as warm or cool depending on the tone and strength of the colour.

We have already seen in Chapter 2 that there are very real reasons why certain colours are termed warm while others are cool. Studies have shown that people have felt physically warmer working in rooms decorated in warm colours, than when working in exactly the same rooms decorated with cool colours, and we will be examining the implications of this further on in the book. This will obviously play a very important role in your design, and when we take a close look at colour psychology in Chapters 8 and 9, all will become clear. In the meantime, there is another way of using warm and cool colours that every designer should fully exploit. I want to show you here how warm and cool colours can be used to create optical illusions.

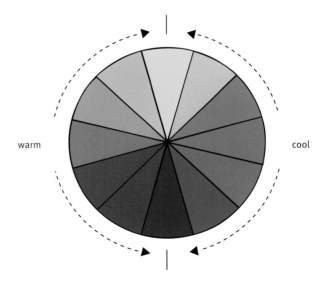

warm   cool

Advancing and receding colours

The way you use colour can dramatically alter the proportions of a room. It is possible to change the apparent height, width and length of a room, simply by the way you use colour and tone. But how does this work?

A colour can make a surface seem closer or further away than it really is, and so look smaller or larger than it actually is. In general, warm colours advance and can be used to make a room seem cosier or more intimate. Darker colours also advance and designers use this characteristic all the time. A favourite trick is in large rooms with high ceilings, where painting the ceiling in a warm or dark colour can visually lower the ceiling and create a more relaxing, comfortable atmosphere.

The other side of the coin is that cool colours tend to recede. In effect, they can be used to 'push back' the walls of a room and so create a more spacious, airy feel. Light colours also recede, and if you wanted to create the maximum illusion of space you could use a cool colour in a light tone to achieve this. These particular characteristics play a very important role in interior design and can be used to great effect:

raising and lowering a ceiling
creating space, making it more cosy
hiding unwanted features, making features stand out
disguising awkward shaped rooms (attics)
widen, shorten or change proportions of a corridor

Please note which colours are warm and which are cool. Many designers become too rigid in their approach, once they have learnt one of the many design 'rules', and this can work to their detriment. Yellow is considered a warm colour in general, but if we look at the colour wheel, yellow-green is on the cool side. This means that a yellow that has any trace of green in it could actually look quite cool, and many of us will have noticed this in practice. In addition to this, many pale colours with a very light tone appear quite cool and have the same characteristics as other cool colours. Even a pale pink (which obviously is based on a warm hue – red) could fall into this category. My reasoning for this, is that when a colour is that light, it will usually contain a high percentage of white in it, and white is a cool 'colour', so to speak.

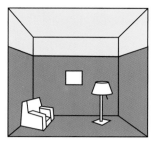

Raising a ceiling.

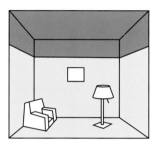

Lowering a ceiling.

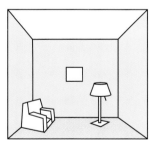

Making a small room
seem larger.

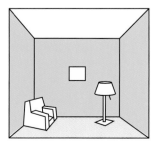

Making a large room
feel smaller.

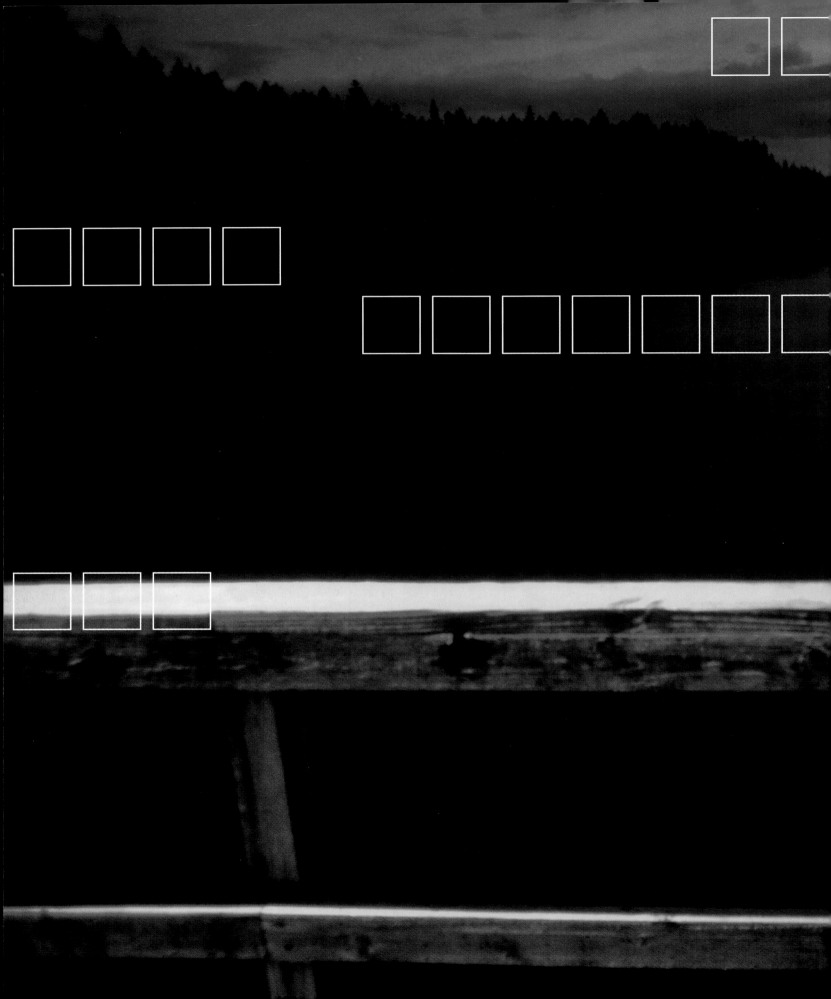

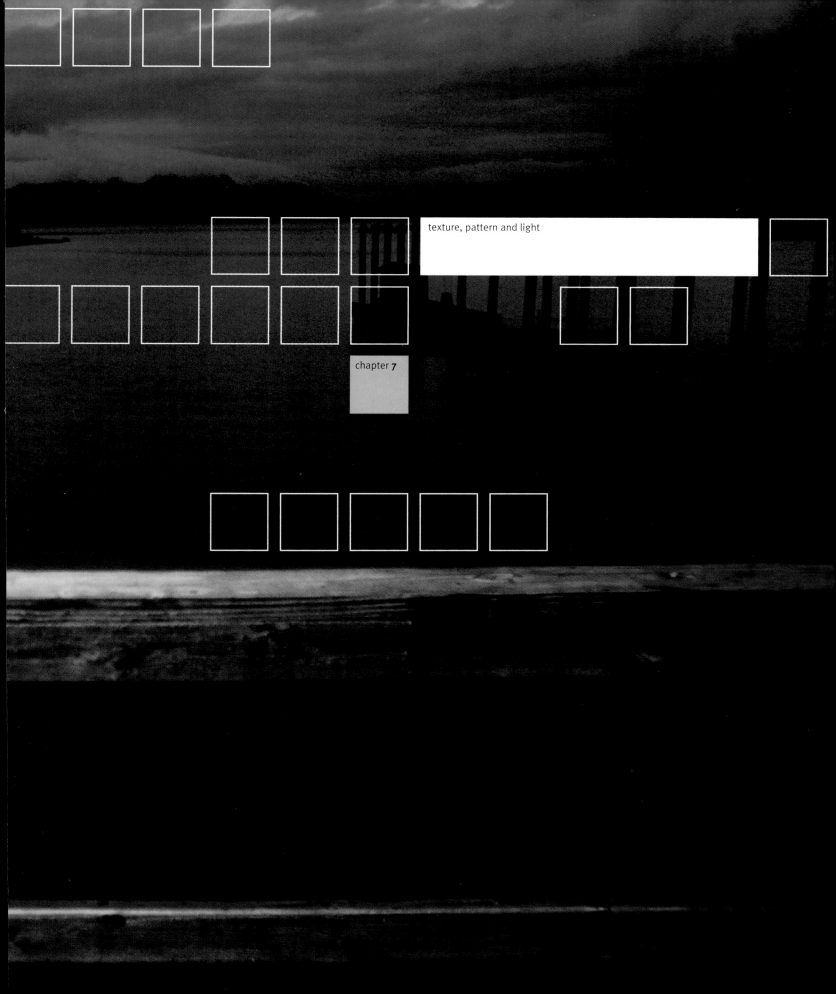

texture, pattern and light

chapter **7**

So far we can see what a wonderful tool colour is in interior design, but even more fabulous effects can be achieved when you introduce texture, pattern and light into a scheme.

Texture

Texture adds another dimension to working with colour and should also be given careful consideration as to the final effect desired. Think of a vibrant emerald green in a crisp cotton fabric, and then imagine the same colour in crushed velvet. Although the colour would be the same, it would look slightly different and the texture would play an important role in the overall feeling that is imparted. Using textured surfaces in interiors can be very effective and can create subtle visual interest, which is very pleasing to the senses. Different textures will not only create different effects, but they will suggest a different mood and feeling.

Take another look at our crisp cotton emerald green fabric. This would probably be best suited to an informal setting. Cotton is usually lightweight and a fresh fabric that lends itself well to short pretty curtains, or long billowing drapes, hung loosely from a curtain pole.

A velvet fabric, however, particularly crushed velvet, has a distinctive air of luxury and richness about it, and a formal setting would be far more suitable. This fabric would never be made into short curtains, but would be elegant as full-length drapes that skim or sit on the floor surface. If they were hung from a pole, it would be a rich mahogany pole with decorative finials, and they would have a deep hand-pleated heading. Naturally, they would be beautifully tied-back so that they always draped elegantly.

Let's look at another example. If you were creating a reading area within your home, leather chairs in any colour, but with a deep buttoned-back upholstery, would help to create a formal setting that is reminiscent of a traditional library. This style would have an air of authority about it. However, large over-stuffed armchairs covered in velvet corduroy would create a more inviting and comfortable feeling. If this was a family area, to be used by children as well as adults, this might be a more appropriate choice. The colours may be exactly the same and both styles could look rich and luxurious, but the final choice of material for the chairs would be decided by the mood and atmosphere that you would like the room to convey.

Many people try to find similar textures when they are putting together a decorative scheme, but wonderful effects can be achieved and you can have a lot of fun by experimenting with contrasting finishes. Sometimes pairing unlikely textures together can bring out the beauty of each one, much in the same way that colour works. Sleek, silky fabrics and lightweight sheers combined with rough linens and knobbly tweeds create a pleasing combination of weaves. Likewise, a rich velvet suite of furniture with plump comfortable cushions would look even more luxurious if it was set off against roughly plastered walls. Putting contrasting textures together like this can create excitement in a scheme, and you should play around and experiment with as many finishes as you can to see how this works.

With the current trend towards minimal interiors, use of textures will become even more important, particularly as many of these schemes use neutral beiges and creams, which can easily become dull and bland if they are not handled properly. When you are working with neutral schemes, the textured surfaces throw strong shadows and glass or metal surfaces reflect light, all of which create the necessary visual interest. Using unusual shapes and forms is also important, and this can create an interesting focal point for the eye. Think of a vase with contorted willow set against a plain background, or a beautifully sculpted vase in a metallic finish. Textures like this can be made even more interesting by the use of carefully selected lighting.

You can clearly see how texture can add interest and variety to a scheme, yet it is very subtle and doesn't distract from the main features. The textures you choose will obviously have an effect on the colour, and generally speaking, matt materials will appear darker, whereas shiny surfaces will reflect the light more and so appear brighter. Some textures can lessen the intensity of a colour and this can be seen to great effect in broken paint techniques. If you want to use a strong colour all the way around a room, but feel it may be overpowering, paint effects can be your best friend. The broken finish gives visual relief to the eye, allowing you to use a strong colour on a large area. One of the major bonuses of this is that paint effects often create a decorative focal point in themselves, and they are very useful in disguising less than perfect walls cheaply and easily.

With so much choice, I'm sure you can see how easy it can be for an untrained person to make mistakes. The key to success is careful planning and experimenting with sample boards, which we will cover in depth in Chapter 10.

Pattern

The definition of pattern is 'a repeated decorative design', whether it be on wallpaper, fabric or carpet, etc. The pattern repeat can be regular and follow a logical order, or it can be a random combination of shapes and colours. I suppose a very coarse definition would be to say that if it's not plain, it's patterned. Pattern offers even more exciting opportunities and ways of working with colour, and there are times indeed when the right pattern and combination of colours can salvage what would seem like a decorating disaster.

When people don't take the time to plan a decor scheme properly, this is when mistakes happen. One of the most common mistakes is a mixture of colours that may have sounded nice initially, but because the scheme hasn't been properly planned, the colours don't really work together in the final result. When it is a case of merely changing the wall colour, many people will decide to just cut their losses and repaint the walls. But what if the mistake has been made with something that is not so easy to change, such as furniture or expensive curtains? If you can manage to find a pattern that combines the same colours within it, then you can make it look as if each item was chosen deliberately. And this is easier than it sounds.

The choice of colours and patterns seems infinite at the moment, and there is bound to be something suitable for any potential problem. But even if you don't see what you want in a wallpaper or fabric, you can create your own style of pattern using a combination of decorative techniques. For walls, any of the broken paint finishes (such as colourwashing, ragging, sponging, etc.) can be made using a combination of colours. Or you can apply pattern on top of a plain wall by using stencilling or stamping techniques, among others. Of course the same thing can be done with curtain fabric. It is also possible to create very simple patterns with fabric by combining two or more fabrics together. By simply bordering curtains in a contrasting colour, the whole effect can be dramatically altered, yet look elegant and simple.

This way of working with pattern offers infinite possibilities, as you choose not only the combination of colours, but the scale and style of the pattern as well. However, there are other ways to get the most out of pattern.

It is very easy to put together an entire decor scheme if you have a patterned wallpaper or fabric to start with, as a popular way of working is to simply pick out the individual colours for other items such as carpeting and furniture. Many interior designers work like this, and amateur decorators can also achieve great success in this way. The main thing is not to get too hung up on finding an exact, precise match in colour. I have often seen people sweating because the shade of apricot in the chair fabric is slightly different from that in the curtains. Once the tone of the colour is correct and the styles combine well together, then that is the most important thing. You will rarely get an exact colour match between two different fabrics or wallpapers etc. Besides which, these items are usually spaced slightly apart and the difference will probably be unnoticeable to most people. This method of planning your decor scheme around a pattern can be extended even further when creating themed rooms.

Last, but by no means least, pattern can be used to suggest a certain period or style. For instance, heraldic motifs make us think of a Gothic style, and Grecian urns and columns make us think of a very classic style. As you can see, there are so many possibilities, but sometimes this can make it easier to make mistakes. So while there are no hard and fast rules, here are a few guidelines to working with pattern:

Always view the pattern in the area you wish to put it from a distance. Some small patterns can merge together on a large area and appear plain.

Generally speaking, keep large scaled patterns to large areas, and smaller patterns on small areas.

When combining patterns together, be careful that the scheme doesn't become overpowering and confusing to the eye, which will cause a restless feeling. It is usually best to combine patterns of different scales if you want to take this approach, but you should experiment a little first by placing samples around the room together and singly to see the best effect.

Patterns tend to lead the eye around the room. Take care to provide a focal point for the eye to rest on so that the scheme does not feel too restless.

When choosing patterned fabrics for curtains, hold them up in front of the window to see how they will look with the light shining through them. This can have a dramatic effect on the way the fabric looks. It is also a good idea to roughly pleat the fabric as it would be in a curtain, as this will change the look quite a bit.

If using several patterns in one room, it is usually best if there is some visual link. Try to choose patterns with colour, texture or some theme in common. The key again is to experiment before committing yourself.

Be careful about the display of objects or pictures against a patterned background. If you want to display something prominently, it is best set against a fairly plain background, as it could be lost against a pattern.

The effect of light on colour

Lighting is a huge area on its own, and there are many factors to be considered when planning your lighting choices. This topic is vast and there are many good books already on this subject, so I will concern myself only with the effect that lighting will have on your colour scheme. You already know that colour is shattered light, so the strong relationship between colour and light is obvious. When planning any scheme it is essential to take into consideration the quality of the light, as this can have dramatic effects on the colour.

Natural lighting is the most obvious type to look at first. Natural daylight will show colours in their true form with no distortion, and it is good to compare colours in natural daylight when you are choosing between shades. However, all colour choices must be viewed in the interior in which they will be placed, as obviously the amount of natural light available will have an effect on the colour.

Although the quality of light that enters a room will depend on whether the room faces south, north, east or west, the main factor will be how many windows allow light into the area. The size of the windows is also important. A penthouse apartment with panoramic view windows will obviously be much brighter than a country cottage with low ceilings and small inset windows. As a result, the same furnishings would look completely different in these settings. Where we are located globally is also an important point. Countries that get quite a lot of sunlight will produce much brighter rooms, whereas in the British Isles, where we tend to have quite gloomy weather, the natural lighting is not very good and rooms can look dull and grey without artificial lighting, even during the day. Seasonal changes are also important, and large modern windows will be more affected by this, as we see in the case of conservatories.

As a designer (and this could be viewed as sacrilege), I don't actually take too much notice of the direction that a room faces. I would obviously take into account the time of day that the sun is strongest and how it would shine into the room, but this would be more from the point of view of shielding furniture and *objets d'art* from the bleaching effect of the sun. If, however, the sun never shines directly through this window, this may not be a problem. Apart from this, I try not to get hung up on whether a room faces due east or south-west. Many designers will argue that if a room faces north it will get very little sunlight and will therefore be cold, so you should never use cool colours, particularly blue. This is (I believe) a good example of how individuals have become too rigid in their approach, and have taken the guidelines of design as golden rules never to be broken. This approach is not only limiting, but through first-hand experience I have seen that it is not always accurate. So the point then, is to assess the amount of natural light that you have coming into the area. If you want to increase the amount of natural light in any area, this can be done in a number of ways:

If it is possible, install larger windows, Velux windows or skylights where necessary.

Glass blocks have become very popular, and these can replace solid walls, allowing light to flood an area and so creating a more spacious feel. Glass blocks have the advantage of still maintaining privacy.

Mirrors can be used to reflect light back into the area and so create the illusion of more space.

In areas where there is no natural light, such as a hall or corridor, decorating the walls with a pale or light colour will not increase the light. If you were decorating a dark hallway, for instance, and were given a choice of pale pink or strong red, most people would choose the pink, assuming that it would be a better choice as the red would make the area seem closed in and dark. Although personal tastes also have to be considered, if the room is naturally dull because of insufficient daylight, the pale pink will not change this. In fact, without sufficient lighting the room will be stripped of its colour and will still appear grey and dull. However, the red walls would be vibrant by comparison and would create a far more striking impression. Either way, the level of light would have to be improved. If it was not possible to increase the amount of natural light, then it would have to be improved artificially.

Artificial lighting in the home used to be limited to standard bulbs with tungsten filament, and these still remain the most popular choice today. However, there have been major improvements in the quality and styles of lighting available. While you will spend most of your effort deciding on the style of fitting and the effects that you wish to create, your choice of bulb will affect the intensity of the colour. Consider these points when making your choices:

Fluorescent lights are most commonly seen in workrooms and kitchens in the home. They are cheap to run and the bulbs last an incredibly long time, but they are not very attractive and the light is quite harsh. When they first came on to the market, fluorescent lights emitted a cool blue or greenish light, which had the effect of stripping colour and creating a draining effect on objects and people. Now, fluorescent bulbs are available with colour correction, and some versions are supposed to simulate daylight. Even though they have improved dramatically, they can still be too harsh on the eyes, and they have a tendency to flicker, which is bad news for people who suffer from headaches. We are all familiar with the conventional tube fluorescent bulbs, and these are also available in smaller versions. These mini-strip lights are commonly used as task lighting underneath wall-mounted cupboards, but they are not usually available in colour-corrected versions.

Tungsten bulbs are still the most popular choice in homes today. They are not particularly energy-efficient, but they are readily available and cheap to replace. They produce a warm light, which is quite close to natural light, but it does tend to emphasise warm colours. However, this is usually quite flattering to people as well as interiors. Tungsten bulbs are now available in a variety of soft tones, where the glass bulb has been tinted to give a softly coloured glow. These can be quite attractive, but it is essential to carefully view your chosen colours under your choice of tinted bulb and in natural daylight.

Candlelight will obviously not be your first choice for main lighting, but the natural flame of a candle or fire can add warmth and atmosphere to a room, and it deserves a mention. This type of light will have little effect on your colour scheme, as the light is usually quite dim, but candles are very popular at the moment for the ambience that they create.

When you approach a new decorating project, there is one very important factor to keep in mind regarding your lighting requirements. Remember that darker colours absorb more of the light rays and will need to be well lit, particularly in the evenings. Paler or lighter coloured rooms will need less lighting for good visibility.

Lighting is not just an obvious necessity, but it can draw attention to decorative details, and it can help to create mood and atmosphere. Of course, colour itself has the largest role to play in creating the right mood, and individual colours commonly produce certain feelings in all of us. If you want to know more about this aspect of colour, then read on to find out about the fascinating subject of colour psychology.

chapter **8**

colour psychology

It is no accident that we use certain colours to describe how we are feeling, such as 'I'm a little blue' or 'I saw red!' As you will see, not only do colours quite accurately describe our moods and emotions, but they also affect them, and in this chapter we will be looking at the specific moods that individual colours create.

Colour psychology is the study of colour and its subsequent effect on the emotions of people. Most of these associations are subconscious, and there are many sceptics that view this subject as hocus-pocus, but in Chapter 2 we looked at how colour is transmitted to the brain as electrical impulses which eventually pass through to the hypothalamus. The hypothalamus, as we know, is the area of the brain that governs our endocrine system, and thereafter our hormones, which are largely responsible for how we feel. This clearly illustrates how everyone is affected by colour and reinforces scientifically what our intuition has been telling us for years. While it is important to remember that we are all individuals and each one of us will react differently to certain colours, in general colour evokes the same feelings and reactions in most people. What's more, this has been found to correspond around the world, and in all cultures.

If colours have such a strong effect on the way we feel, doesn't it then make sense that we should consider colour psychology when we are deciding on a colour scheme? After all, if we are to be surrounded by these colours in our homes and workplaces, the effect they will have on us over a long period of time is incredibly important. But which colours do you choose?

Red

Red is the most powerful colour of the spectrum, and
psychologically it can both attract and repel, depending
on the emotional state and beliefs of the individual. It is
a colour that creates excitement and has always been
associated with courage and power. Symbolically, red
has always been worn by the leader, the person who
takes action. It is the colour of royalty and symbolises
power around the world. It makes sense then, that we
roll out the red carpet for our VIPs and royalty.

As it is the colour of blood, many primitive cultures
regard red as the life force within each of us. Red is
connected to the release of adrenalin within our bodies,
which in turn is responsible for our 'fight or flight' reflex.
Thus it has always been linked with fighting and war,
and has been used throughout history to represent
military power. The colour of the Roman legions,
probably the greatest army that we have ever seen, was
of course, 'Pompeii' red.

Red is the colour of fire and passion, and it represents
our desires and cravings in all areas – power, food and
sex. It is the colour most often associated with sexuality,
and the Eastern beliefs relate red to the base chakra and
the reproductive organs. In the West it is associated
with love, the romantic side of sex. Red hearts on
Valentine's Day and red roses at any time have an
obvious significance.

Red has the longest wavelength of all the colours in the
spectrum and requires the most adjustment from the
eyes. This is why it can be seen as a stressful colour,
and it has actually been shown to increase the heart
rate and blood pressure, so use it with caution.

Positive characteristics: Red shows leadership and is not afraid to make a statement. It is dynamic and self-confident, and symbolises power and drive. Red does not hide, it is a public colour that believes in action and is courageous and passionate. The Red Cross rescuers are a good example of how to use the positive attributes of this colour. Red never seems tired, it keeps on moving. It can be used to ignite passions, romantically or theoretically speaking. In interior design, there are many places where red can be used positively:

In any room or building where increased physical activity is required. It is good for corridors and places where you want to keep people moving.

It has been shown to stimulate the appetite and conversation, so it is an ideal choice for restaurants and dining rooms.

Associated with power and wealth, it is an ideal colour to use in ceremonial or state rooms, where a grand atmosphere is required. On a lesser scale, it can also be used to invoke the same feelings in jewellers or other shops where luxury items are being sold.

As the hottest colour of the spectrum, it can make anywhere seem warm and cosy, so can be ideal for people who suffer from the cold.

Negative characteristics: Red can sometimes be seen as overpowering and pushy. Red rushes in without thinking, and can be prone to violence, hence the sayings, 'hot-headed' and 'red with rage'. As red is used for warning signs around the world, it signals danger to many people and can put them on their guard. These same people might view red as domineering and defiant, and would often associate it with showing off. While it is associated with love and sexuality, the wrong tones can have an adverse effect and are often viewed as lustful and perverse. Red has always been associated with harlots and prostitutes – I'm sure you've all heard of the red light district! Taking these things into consideration, there are some places where it would not be suitable to use red:

It is not a good choice where calmness and clear thinking are required. In customer service areas or reception areas, it can be overpowering and claustrophobic, which in turn can create hostility and increase irritability.

Its energetic frequency is not conducive to areas where rest is needed, so it is not a good choice for bedrooms or relaxation areas.

Where concentration is needed it should be avoided, in studies or in areas where potentially dangerous machinery is in operation.

Because it can increase feelings of stress and irritation, it should not be used where people are spending long periods of time, particularly in office situations where they have to sit in one place. Overexposure to red has been shown to cause headaches.

It must be absolutely avoided in places where there are likely to be hyperactive or violent adults or children. As a stimulating colour, it will only stimulate this anti-social behaviour even more.

For the above reason, red is not a good choice for public houses or drinking establishments.

It should not be used in areas where people suffer from any type of heart conditions, blood pressure, or inflammatory problems.

A word about pink: Although the colour pink has a red base, it has a completely different effect than the colour red, and is essentially used as a calming colour. It is traditionally associated with love and romance, whereas red is associated with sex – a much stronger force. It is used in industry to create a gentle environment, and it is probably for this reason that it is associated with women and the softer, feminine personality. At home it is a good choice for bedrooms, and can be balanced with blues or greens and used in muted tones so that it does not appear too feminine.

Orange

Orange is a warm, vibrant colour and is psychologically
linked to health and vitality. Orange brings together the
properties of red and yellow, and while it has the
strength and tireless energy of red, this is combined
with the mental clarity and wisdom of yellow. In effect,
this makes orange a more practical colour. It doesn't
rush in without thinking, but it is constructive and likes
to get things done. Whereas red demands attention,
orange is merely persistent. The happiness and joy of
yellow also blends well in orange to make a more
sociable and optimistic colour, that likes to work as
part of a team.

Symbolically, orange is regarded as a positive colour,
that raises tolerance and strengthens will – which is
probably why Buddhist monks choose to wear orange
robes. Some yogis call this colour the 'soul of energy',
and in Japan, it is the colour of love and happiness.
Representing the sacral chakra, and the adrenals and
kidneys, it evokes secondary survival instincts and is
connected with physical enjoyment. It is associated with
strength and endurance, and is the colour attributed to
Zeus, the supreme ruler of the gods in Greek mythology.
It is a good colour for sportspeople and athletes, and for
people with sexual difficulties.

Orange does not allow you to sit still. Instead, it
provokes change and stirs up dormancy. In spite of all
its positive qualities, orange is not a popular colour and
may be rejected by people, so you should think carefully
before you opt to use it.

Positive characteristics: Orange is strong and flamboyant, yet it is equally warm-hearted and generous. It is an enthusiastic, positive colour that keeps on going. It is a good colour for self-awareness and self-expression, yet it is sociable and likes to work in groups. Orange is red, but without the aggressive force. It is a colour that helps to assimilate new ideas and brings freedom from material limitations. It is good to use in any place that needs cheering up, and in creative fields. The following areas would all be suitable places to use orange:

It is a very good colour to use with children. As well as making children more sociable and cheerful, it has been shown to improve academic performance.

Autistic children in particular respond very well to this colour, and it helps to develop abilities that are blocked.

Sportspeople relate to orange and it is particularly good for exercise rooms, sports halls or playrooms.

Its creative and constructive qualities make it a particularly good choice for designers, architects, and similar creative industries.

It helps increase the appetite, so would again be a good choice for a restaurant or dining room.

It would also be a good colour for public houses and social centres.

Psychological therapists have found that it can help in cases of mental breakdown and depression, so it would be a good choice for consulting rooms.

Negative characteristics: Orange is probably one of the most unpopular colours, and is often rejected by people. It represents change, and the majority of people feel insecure when they don't know what lies ahead. In traffic signals, orange is used to caution people; but doesn't make a clear statement like red or green, so it can be seen as misleading. It can be seen as over-proud and self-indulgent. Some tones can be cheap and it can be seen as a show-off. Its persistence can be annoying, and sometimes it may not know when to stop. There are some places where orange should definitely be avoided:

It is not suitable for rest rooms or areas of relaxation.

It should be avoided if you tend to overeat and drink, or suffer from addictions.

In places where there are likely to be hyperactive or irritable people.

In places where people might suffer from nausea.

Yellow

Yellow is the colour of sunshine and happiness, and very few people dislike this colour or the effect that it creates. As it is also from the warm side of the spectrum, it is a stimulating and energetic colour, yet it does not distract and has been shown to improve mental clarity and verbal reasoning. Yellow is an emotional colour, and is more often associated with joy, but it has been shown to create feelings of anxiety in some people and can cause butterflies in the tummy. This could be why we relate the colour yellow to fear, and how we got the sayings, 'yellow streak' and 'yellow journalism'. Appropriately, the Eastern beliefs relate yellow to the solar plexus chakra, and the stomach area, which is also seen as the seat of our emotions.

Symbolically, yellow represents the life-giving sun, the source of all life on earth, so it is another colour associated with power. In imperial China, only the emperor was allowed to wear yellow, and it continues to represent nobility in the East. As a highly visible colour, it is extrovert in nature and focuses on the ego. It is closely linked with our feelings of self-esteem and personal power.

Yellow is generally seen as a light, optimistic colour, and has a unique ability to raise the spirits and inject vitality into any area. It also has a quick and original mind, which shows great insight and good use of intellectual abilities. Although yellow is strongly connected with creative energy, over-use of yellow can suggest a disturbed mind.

Positive characteristics: Yellow is a highly visible colour, and not good at hiding things, so it would usually be seen as honest and confident. As the sun shines equally on everyone on the earth, yellow is also seen as having a generous nature. Being so closely linked to sunlight, it is an excellent colour to lift the spirits and would work well in the following places:

It creates a warm and welcoming first impression in halls and reception areas.

A good colour to use with depressed people, it is well suited for doctors' and, in some cases, counsellors' consulting rooms.

A good choice for children's playrooms to stimulate their creativity.

It has long been a favourite for kitchens as it sets the mood for the rest of the day and helps creativity and conversation.

Yellow aids mental clarity and is a good choice for studies and workrooms.

As most people are positively affected and feel optimistic, yellow is a good colour to use in sales areas, particularly sales offices.

High visibility makes it a good choice for signs and shop fronts, or any area that you wish to draw attention to.

Negative characteristics: The most negative points about yellow are that it is strongly associated with fear and with sickness. We've all heard of yellow jaundice, and yellow is also the colour of the flag of quarantine. When yellow becomes green it can be particularly sickly. This is the colour of bile, and many people have a strong negative reaction to these shades. You will rarely see the colour yellow used in airports or airplanes, probably because of its connection with both sickness and fear. It has also been associated with hate and jealousy, and is the colour of venom. These are strong negative qualities, and so there are definite places where yellow is to be avoided:

It is not a good choice for a restaurant or dining room. The yellow-green shades in particular must be completely avoided.

Although it is a popular choice for bedrooms, these would usually be pastel yellows, and they still need careful balancing. Stronger variations should be avoided in bedrooms, particularly for people who suffer from insomnia.

Avoid using it in areas where children or adults suffer from hyperactivity.

It should not be used in areas where people might show aggressive behaviour or tendencies.

Yellow should never be used in areas where you might be dealing with emotionally disturbed people, or where people might be upset, such as customer service departments.

It should be avoided in areas where people have been commonly shown to express fear, such as dentists' waiting rooms and airports.

Green

Green is the colour of nature. It surrounds us in
everyday life, and it is the colour of balance and
harmony. Green shoots on plants indicate new growth
and hope, and so green symbolises fertility in many
cultures. A down-to-earth and practical colour, the green
stem of the flower connects the bloom above with the
roots below. It displays friendliness, co-operation, and a
generous love for all things natural, and this is why it is
so often chosen to suggest a return to nature. I'm sure
we are all aware of the move towards 'green thinking',
the Green political party, Greenpeace, etc. It is often
connected to the idealistic attitudes we see in our
youth, hence we often refer to young, inexperienced
people as 'green'. This aspect of green unfortunately
means that it is not always taken seriously, and so it can
be a bad colour to choose when you need to show or
express authority.

Symbolically, green represents the heart chakra and is
associated with our ability to love in the universal sense,
but it is also connected with our jealousies. Hence we
have the sayings, 'the green-eyed monster' and 'green
with envy'. Green is abundant in nature and it has also
come to be associated with prosperity in the material
world. As green is the colour of money and of the
economist, an over-use of green can be associated with
greed and miserliness.

Essentially, green combines the wisdom of yellow with
the truthfulness and trustworthiness of blue. It is mid-
way between the colours of the spectrum and the
chakra points on the body, bridging the gap between the
mind and the spirit. Green can see both sides and has
its feet firmly on the ground, therefore it makes the right
judgement. It is a good colour for balance and making
decisions. Green requires the least adjustment of the
eyes, and so it is a restful and refreshing colour, and is
ideal for areas of relaxation. Many invalids are sent to
the country to convalesce where they can be surrounded
by greenery, and it is a wonderfully healing colour.

Although I know many designers who might be horrified
by this statement, green is the one colour in the
spectrum (apart from neutrals), that works with any
other colour, and most rooms can benefit from even
small additions of healing green. Mother Nature
provides the best inspiration of all, and there are
millions of beautifully coloured flowers in the world, yet
none of them ever clash with the green leaves that
surround them!

Positive characteristics: Green is a very healing, soothing colour, and although it is not suited to all businesses, it can be used to create a relaxing area in any part of the home. In cities and towns in particular, people always feel refreshed after spending some time surrounded by grass and trees in a park, and adding greenery to an interior, is an easy way of benefiting from the properties of this colour. Its no-nonsense attitude makes it practical and productive, and it is known for having a generous nature. A good colour for balance, it makes the right decisions, but it also complements this by being supportive and tactful when necessary. These strong, positive characteristics make green a good choice of colour for many areas:

It is wonderful to use in hospitals or clinics, and is particularly good for people who suffer from heart or inflammatory conditions. It also aids relief of skin disorders and allergies, and has been used to treat serious burns.

If you suffer from auto-immune problems, asthma or bronchitis, green can aid relief.

It is excellent for treating shock and chronic fatigue.

Green helps treat hyperactivity in children and adults, and restores a calm environment.

It would be a particularly good choice for customer service areas or complaints departments of large companies or firms.

As it adds calmness, it can be good to use in industrial areas that would otherwise seem hostile and cold, taking energy from the occupants. Green would add balance.

Its down-to-earth approach and generous nature make it trustworthy, and therefore a good colour for charities and other worthwhile causes.

Green's ability to make balanced decisions means that it is particularly well suited to offices where important choices have to be made relating to individuals, such as social workers and personnel departments.

Negative characteristics: Green is seen in many places as unlucky. Before the advent of modern medicine, cuts and accidents that turned limbs green showed gangrene, and meant that the limb had to be removed, so this could be one reason why. It can also represent our jealousies, and can be seen as resentful and greedy. Green likes to plough ahead and get things done, but this can sometimes result in frustration when things don't work out, and it can be seen as self-righteous and proud, rather than determined. Naturally there are places were green would not be recommended:

It should not be used in areas where people suffer from laziness and lack of motivation.

Some shades of green can cause nausea, and it would not be the best choice for dining rooms or restaurants.

Not seen as having authority, green is not taken seriously in business and should not be used in managers' offices, boardrooms, or in areas that need to project an official air.

It is not a good choice for studies, laboratories or places where detached, analytical thinking is required.

Green should not be used in areas where you want to keep people moving. In staff relaxation areas, for example, the use of green might encourage employees to linger rather than get back to work.

Blue

The last of the primary colours, blue is the voice of calm and reason. It is rational and clear-thinking, and speaks confidently with truth and wisdom. Blue has a spiritual side to its nature, and it is continually questioning, searching for the meaning of life. It keeps an open mind, looking for the answers in both science and religion, yet the intellectual side of blue demands logic and requires that all answers can be reasonably argued. These sound like high expectations, and rightfully so, because blue has high ideals and promotes self-expression and personal responsibility. Coincidentally, the Eastern beliefs relate light blue to the throat chakra, responsible for verbal communication, and dark blue to the brow chakra. This is also known as the third eye and supposedly governs our intuition and spiritual insight.

The many variations of blue range from the pale blue of a summer sky to the rich, deep blue of a beautiful sapphire, which may explain why it is the world's favourite colour. Richer shades of blue have a strong sense of occasion and are often associated with royalty, which is probably why we refer to the aristocracy as those with blue blood in their veins. In addition to its connection with nobility, blue is also symbolic of peace and devotion. Appropriately enough, the Christian faiths have always associated it with the Virgin Mary, who besides being the Mother of Christ, is often depicted as the 'Queen of Heaven'. Tranquil and serene in its nature, it is the colour of contemplation and inner reflection, and in fact most religions throughout the world use blue as one of their symbolic colours.

Blue is not a demanding colour. Instead, its cool and reserved nature recedes into the background, and it doesn't like to draw attention to itself. This characteristic, combined with its high ideals, can lead some people to think of blue as cold and snobbish, and it can also be mistaken as unfriendly because of its tendency to be introspective. Unfortunately, this aspect of blue often creates feelings of isolation, leading in turn to sadness and depression. If you find this doubtful at all, just ask yourself if you've ever suffered from 'the blues' at one time or another.

On a more positive note, blue generally represents sincerity and loyalty, and dark blue in particular is very conscientious and reliable in a crisis. It conveys authority, and is a popular choice in businesses generally, and for official uniforms such as the police. Associated with a strong, but calm personality, blue is a truly dignified colour.

Positive characteristics: In the heat of the moment, blue remains calm and clear-thinking. It has many positive qualities, not least its wisdom and honesty. Blue has strong healing powers, and blue light is commonly used in hospitals as an antiseptic, and to treat new-born babies suffering from jaundice. It has been shown to reduce fevers and inflammation, and has also been successfully used to treat burns. Blue's calm and restful nature can act as a potent sedative, making it a good colour for anyone with sleeping difficulties. It also helps to combat fear, and can encourage people to speak up for themselves. It has been shown to relieve tension headaches and lower blood pressure, making it a good antidote for the strains and stresses of modern-day life. Blue would be ideal to use in any of the following areas:

Use it in any area where you want people to cool down, physically or mentally. It is particularly good to use in areas where people are placed under high levels of stress.

It is the perfect choice for use in sickrooms and recovery rooms.

Blue is an ideal colour for bedrooms or rest rooms of any kind.

It is well suited to studies and areas where analytical thinking is required. This would also make it appropriate for most commercial offices.

Blue's ability to encourage clear thought and communication, makes it ideal for boardrooms and other areas where group decisions or brainstorming sessions take place.

Richer shades of blue can be used to create a sense of occasion, while still creating an official atmosphere. This makes it a good choice for official ceremonial rooms and business meeting rooms.

It is a good choice for people trying to combat phobias, and is ideal for places where fear is commonplace, such as dentists' waiting rooms or airports.

Negative characteristics: Blue is reserved in its nature and has a tendency to recede into the background, which can be seen as cold and stand-offish. It has high ideals, but it can expect too much and it is sometimes harsh and unforgiving. Blue can take loyalty to extremes and is often misled by blind devotion, thus it can be seen as weak and emotionally unstable. Like the sea that it represents, blue can be calm and peaceful one minute, yet rocky and turbulent the next. For this reason blue is prone to moodiness, and it is not a very sociable colour. All things considered, there are some places where blue should be avoided:

Blue should not be used in large areas that are hard to heat, and should be avoided by anyone who suffers from the cold.

It should be avoided by anyone who suffers from depression or sadness.

Blue increases feelings of isolation and should be avoided by anyone suffering mental illness or eating disorders.

It is not a good colour for playrooms or areas of physical activity. In fact, it encourages lethargy and should not be used in any areas where you want to create a motivating atmosphere.

Although blue encourages sleep, it should be avoided if you suffer from nightmares.

Blue doesn't like to draw attention to itself, and is not a good colour to use in sales or advertising areas.

Purple

The creativity and physical energy of red combine with the spirituality and intellect of blue to create a very powerful colour that brings together the body and mind. Purple is the colour of true greatness and it is associated with inspired leadership. Symbolically, the person that wears purple should exhibit high levels of mental and emotional balance, and show a love of truth and all that is good. Because of this, no doubt, purple has been chosen as the emblematic colour of various leaders throughout the churches, particularly the bishops of the Christian faith. On the same note, the Eastern beliefs associate purple with the crown chakra, which is the source of all our thoughts and is related to the highest levels of spiritual evolution.

The fiery nature of red gives purple its passion and courage. But whereas red represents our physical cravings, purple represents our spiritual desires, and it seeks to fulfil itself mentally with the finer things in life. Thus, purple has come to represent sensitivity, good taste and a liking for the arts. It is an inspirational colour, full of original and sound ideas, and artists and philosophers relate well to purple. In fact, Leonardo da Vinci himself recommended meditation under purple light, to increase inspiration and mental clarity. However, while it is wonderful for introspection and meditation, this can also lead to feelings of fear and isolation, and purple has been linked with delusional thinking and depression. For the Victorians, purple was symbolic as a colour of mourning.

Generally speaking, few people have reached the high spiritual level that purple represents, and so it remains an unpopular colour that is often misunderstood. While there is no doubt that purple commands respect and is seen in high places, stronger versions can be vibrant and demanding, and many people see purple as pompous and overbearing. For them, purple would be seen as suffering from delusions of grandeur, with an egotistical nature. It seems fitting then that the Roman emperors were notorious for this colour, as all others were forbidden to wear it.

Positive characteristics: Purple is a very inspirational colour, and is a good choice for anyone working in creative fields, particularly those that require solitude for inspiration, such as musical composers, poets, painters and sculptors, etc. It has always had strong associations with the church and royalty, and is generally seen as a grand colour that creates a strong sense of occasion. Purple has come to be associated with dignity and age, and although it is not always possible, purple strives for perfection in all things. Like the best inspirational leader, purple is kind, but never weak, and this seems to make it a good colour for curbing violent anti-social behaviour. Although it requires careful handling in interiors, purple is a striking colour, and its characteristics make it suitable to use in the following places:

As it connects the mind, body and spirit, purple is a good colour for meditation areas or relaxation rooms. It would also be well suited to alternative healing centres and the like.

It is a good colour to use if you are striving for meaning and purpose in life, as it will help you to think clearly and with insight.

Use purple in any area where you want to be inspired – artistically, creatively or spiritually.

It would also be a good choice for religious buildings or rooms where groups congregate to practise their faith.

Purple can help to bring your leadership qualities to the front, so it is a good colour for the offices of chief executives or managing directors. It would also be well suited to someone who is self-employed.

Purple's sense of occasion creates a grand atmosphere, which makes it a good colour for retail outlets selling luxury goods. It also works particularly well with gold, so it would be a good choice for jewellery stores.

Negative characteristics: Purple is a heavy colour, so if it is used, it should be used sparingly. It has been shown to cause depression, and can even bring out suicidal tendencies in emotionally unstable people, which does not make it a very sociable colour. Its introspective nature can exaggerate feelings of loneliness, and in some individuals it will encourage delusional thinking. Purple's aim is to lead, and therefore its social position is very important. It is a social climber, and can be pompous and self-important, so people can view it as fraudulent and ruthless. Taking all of this into account, there are some places where purple is definitely to be avoided:

It is not a very sociable colour and should be avoided in areas where you wish to entertain people. The hospitality industry should avoid using purple, particularly restaurants, pubs or social centres.

Purple's heavy and depressing nature is not suited to use in children's rooms.

It should be avoided in areas where there are mentally ill patients or people suffering from delusions.

People that suffer from addictive disorders, particularly those involving alcohol or drugs, should also avoid it.

If you feel lonely or alienated, purple will only intensify feelings of isolation.

It is not a good colour for businesses that work on trust, such as banks, solicitors, etc.

Avoid purple if you suffer from nightmares or if you fear the paranormal.

Black, white and grey

Strictly speaking, black, white and grey are not actually colours in themselves, as they are not represented on the colour wheel, but they obviously have an important role to play in your colour scheme, and they also have strong psychological associations for most of us.

Black results from the extinction of all light and colour. Pure black is rarely found in nature, and it has strong associations with the world of the supernatural and the occult. For many people it represents darkness, witchcraft and evil, and it is often associated with grief, mourning and penitence. In movies, the bad guys nearly always wear black. It is the colour we link most with death and depression, and when we feel there is no hope we often say, 'the outlook is black'.

In direct contrast to this, some people see black as dark and mysterious. In the Eastern philosophy of Feng Shui, black is powerful and represents money. Black has almost become a uniform in the world of design, and in Western fashion, black is seen as the height of sophistication and glamour.

There is limited use for black in interior design, but it is mainly used to highlight other colours and to define specific areas or items. Using black on a large scale can be very oppressive, but careful balancing with other colours can lend an air of sophistication to a scheme. Black can bring out the beauty of other colours in a scheme, and adding touches of black can create drama. Many teenagers go through a period when they want to decorate their room black, and this usually corresponds with the time when they are going through an identity crisis and trying to discover who they really are.

White represents an equal combination of all the colours of the spectrum present in white light. It is probably because of this that white is seen as a 'well-balanced' colour, which seeks to be pure and fair. Hence the judges in traditional courts wear a white wig to show their impartiality.

Symbolically, white is often representative of a saviour, spiritual or otherwise, and many young girls dream of being rescued by a white knight on his white horse. Most doctors and medical staff also wear white coats, as a sign of health and hygiene foremost, but also as they have come to save us from sickness.

White is open and light, and its nature is pristine and efficient. Because of this it has been adopted as the colour of health and hygiene around the globe, and white has always been a popular choice for hospitals and laboratories. White reflects light and brightens up dark corners. It instantly shows up any imperfection, thus it also represents purity and innocence. It's not surprising that it is the bridal and baptismal colour in so many cultures.

Like all colours, white also has negative aspects. And while the white dove is seen positively as a symbol of peace, the white flag of truce signals surrender – thus white is sometimes seen negatively as the colour of submission. As the colour of winter, white can be cold and hostile, and because it shows up every imperfection, white can also be harsh and unforgiving. Many people see white as sterile and stark, and over-use causes frustration, isolation and feelings of emptiness.

White has always been popular in interior design, as it instantly brightens up any area, and gives the decorator a blank canvas on which to work. While most minimal interiors are based on white schemes, they require extreme tidiness to look good, so they can be very hard to live with and tend to create a clinical atmosphere. If you decide to use white on a large scale, it is better to pick a soft white or cream to prevent the atmosphere from becoming too stark or sterile, and add balance using natural materials where possible, such as wood or natural stone. Generally speaking, white needs other colours to create any sort of mood, and white is usually used to highlight specific areas (particularly display areas), or to draw attention to other decorative details.

In the business world, white is still commonly used to suggest cleanliness and efficiency, mainly by companies that are involved in food preparation or medical services, such as opticians or chemists. Even so, the decor scheme is usually balanced out by other decorative details in contrasting colours and textures. Many large open buildings, such as factories and airports, still choose white as the main decorative finish, but as colour psychology takes on a larger role in interior design, we are thankfully moving away from this particular use.

Grey is associated with old age, for obvious reasons, and also with the wisdom that old age supposedly brings, which is why we refer to intelligent people as having their fair share of 'grey matter'. By the same token, grey is also used to represent confusion, and we talk of a 'grey area' when facts are unclear. True to character, even the psychological associations of grey seem to be confused and contradictory. Grey is the colour of stone and of steel, both solid and dependable materials. While on the one hand, this can be seen as firm and dignified, on the other hand it can be seen as hard and inflexible. No doubt this is one reason why grey has strong links with bureaucracy and institutions.

For the most part, grey is considered to be a dull, lifeless colour, and we often refer to people as 'grey-faced' when they look ill and below par. Over-use of grey can be oppressive and can subdue personality, which is why it is the colour most often chosen for uniforms. Grey is used to make us conform with our environment, as it does itself. Grey's ability to disappear into the background makes it good for camouflage, but it will not attract attention, and in some lights and climates it will not be seen at all. Although it is usually seen as the colour of industrial premises, this makes it a particularly bad colour for businesses. Not only will it create a depressing atmosphere for staff employed there, but it will do nothing to sell the business to others.

In interiors, grey has no personality of its own, and it requires other colours to bring it to life. It is a neutral colour available in many variations, all of which will work with any other colour of the spectrum. Grey is generally used as an accent colour, or as a background for other strong colours, which may need to be toned down and subdued. If grey is used extensively throughout an interior, it can be oppressive and depressing. But carefully balanced, it can bring out the best qualities of the other colours of the spectrum.

Colour psychology is powerful stuff, and it's about time that it made its way into the design industry, where interior designers have the responsibility of helping clients to choose which colours to surround themselves with in their homes and workplaces. However, it is still important to remember, that while colour generally evokes the same feelings in most people, we are all individuals, and each one of us will react differently to certain colours, depending on our own emotional state, beliefs and personal preferences. If you are decorating your own personal space, allow your intuition to guide you more than anything else, but naturally, consider the psychological implications of painting your bedroom in hot red. While your love life may benefit from the excitement, you will probably never get a good night's sleep with this colour.

In business situations, where a company wishes to project a certain image, the psychology obviously takes on a more important role. But even then, you must consider that the information in this section is not absolute, and is not written in stone. The first rule of interior design is that there are no rules, and the most important thing to remember, when designing a scheme, is to create something that is harmonious. Colour psychology is a powerful tool that can be used to create specific moods, but it is not a panacea for all ills. If the tones of different colours and all the other elements of the design are not compatible with each other, the end result will have a negative effect, regardless of the colours chosen. This is still only one of the tools to be used when designing an interior. That said, in the hands of the interior designer, this tool can and has been used to create incredible results.

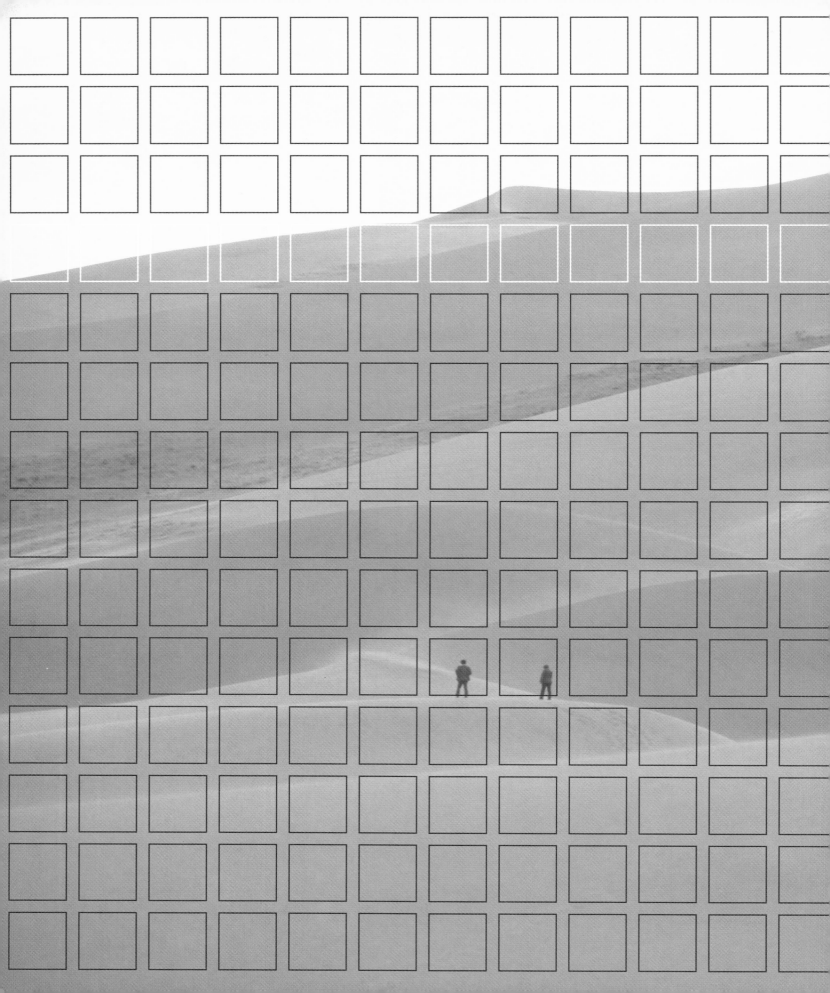

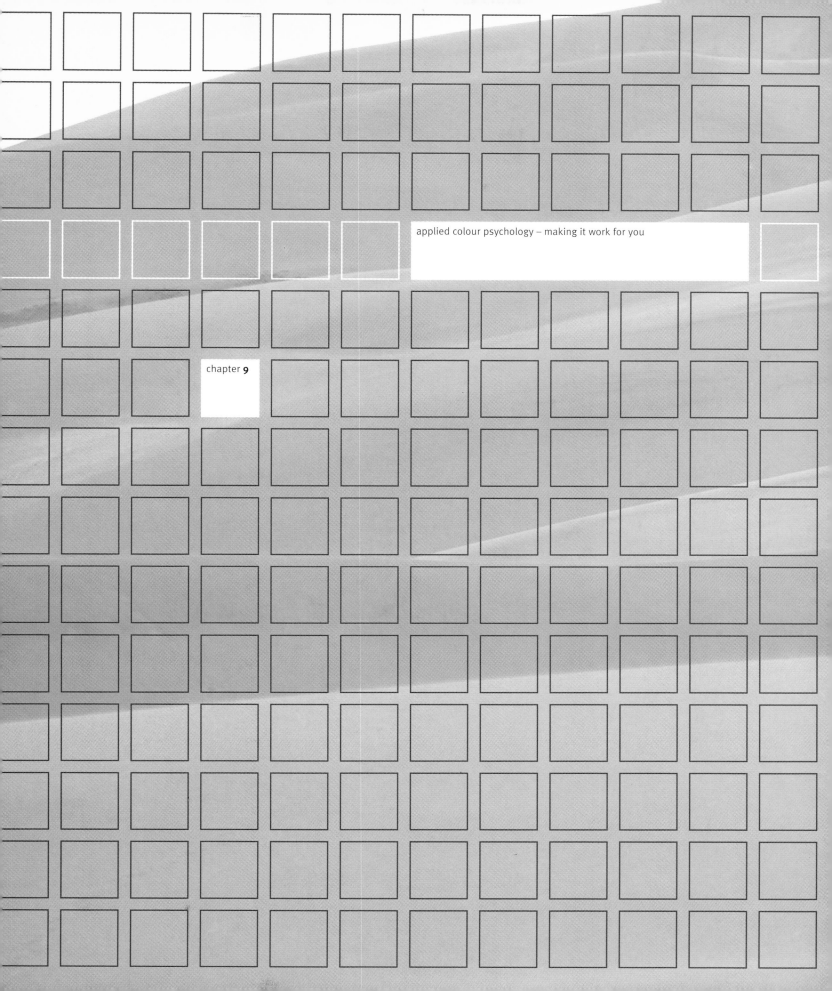

applied colour psychology – making it work for you

chapter **9**

For anyone interested in colour and design, the whole area of colour psychology is naturally fascinating and appealing, and the fact that you are reading this book indicates that you are probably one of those people. For the most part though, claims about how colour can affect our quality of life and even the profitability of our businesses, bring out the sceptic in us, and few people really believe that the colour you paint your walls is that important. Even when I explain to people that this is a proven science and not the latest fad, the majority already have their minds closed, so I often ask them to consider a few simple questions:

'Would you paint your three-year-old's bedroom black?'

'Would you decorate the boardroom of your office in "Barbie" pink?'

'How about a room that you want to unwind in at the end of the day? Could you relax in a room that was decorated entirely in primary red, with red curtains and furniture?'

Very quickly people are forced to admit that colour is more important than they might have initially realised, and although these are extreme examples, they clearly illustrate the point that colours are important to all of us. Once people can approach the subject with an open mind, they quickly become fascinated with a topic that can seem almost magical at times. But let's be realistic, fascinating and interesting is one thing, what about practicality? Is this knowledge really of any value to us?

The answer is a resounding yes. As individuals and businesses around the world are discovering, applying this knowledge can produce truly miraculous results. This information is so valuable that you really can't afford to be without it.

Although research in the area of colour psychology has been continuing since the beginning of this century, the information has not been centralised and it can be quite difficult to obtain. Within the entire field of psychology, this is such a small area that it has become highly specialised, with only a handful of colour consultants operating around the world. As businesses and individuals have begun to discover the impact that this powerful tool can have, they have looked for solutions by seeking out these colour consultants to advise them appropriately – but there is a snag. While each of these professionals would no doubt be very knowledgeable in their own area, they can only advise on colours, and few of them (if any) would have the design expertise necessary to incorporate those colours into a successful interior scheme. Disharmony within an interior has a negative effect, no matter what colours are present, and defeats the entire purpose, so this situation is far from ideal. To combat this, colour consultants have previously worked alongside interior designers, to successfully achieve their desired outcome. But why not just hire a designer who understands colour psychology in the first place? Well from now on, that's probably what will be the case.

Until now, the information available on colour psychology in general has been very hard to come by, but even more so when it is narrowed down to one distinct area, such as interior design. The purpose of this book is to change that, and to present the information in a format that you can easily use. More importantly, it is my hope that you will combine this knowledge with the complete set of design skills, so that you can provide a complete design package for yourself or your client. Undoubtedly, the designer who can do this successfully will be a very valuable asset to their clients, particularly in the business world, where results are so drastic. For this reason, much of the focus of this chapter is on the practical application of colour in industry, but the lessons can be applied to our homes and personal spaces with equal success.

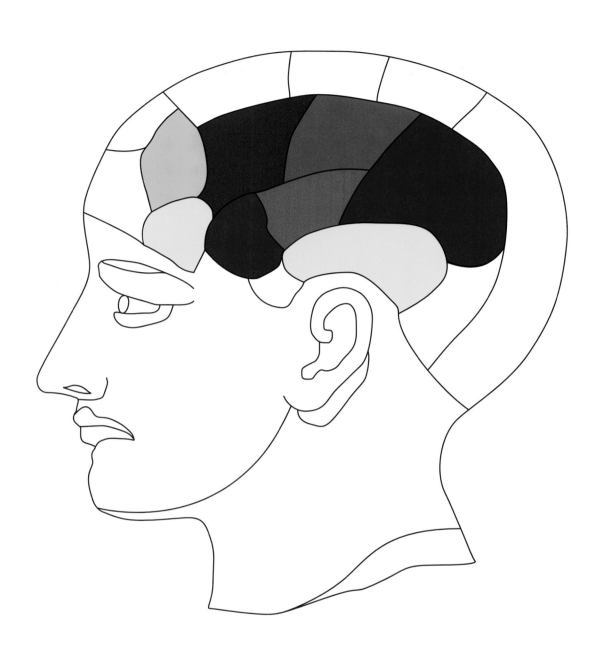

Increasing sales and turnover

Increasing sales and turnover is the fastest way for any business to see an immediate rise in its profits, and the results can be easily measured. By choosing the right colours to display and complement a company's product, the product will instantly look more attractive, and this can have an incredible impact on sales. A well-known case is that of a meat packing house in Chicago, which actually tripled its sales by applying colour psychology. The business wasn't doing as well as anticipated, and a colour consultant was called in to see if anything could be done. It was quickly discovered that the existing yellow walls had been causing a grey after-image, and this was reflected on to the meat, detracting from its appearance. We have already seen how complementary colours intensify each other, and the simple solution in this instance was to paint the walls green. The new green walls made the meat appear redder than ever, and more appealing to customers, hence an immediate impact on sales and profits.

Apologies for stating the obvious here, but I would just like to clarify a point. The key to increasing sales with colour is not necessarily to use the complementary colour to the product on display, but to use colours that will create the best effect and make the product look good. (Remember the effect of simultaneous contrast in Chapter 6.) In the above situation, it is quite obvious that red meat will sell more than meat that is greyed or 'off'-looking. Therefore, green is the natural choice to intensify the red colour of the meat even more, and that is why you will often see plastic greenery placed beside meat displays in supermarkets.

This example clearly shows how the correct colour can help a business to increase its profits, and likewise, ignoring colour psychology when planning the scheme can lose money for a business. Admittedly, solutions such as this are not always quite so straightforward. Retail outlets, in particular, that may need to display a variety of products in different styles and colours, will require a little more thought and creativity, but taking the time to evaluate each situation on its own merits will help you to get it right first time. When you are designing a retail interior always keep in mind the consumer that you are trying to reach, the products that you are trying to sell, and which colours and style will most effectively bring the two together. It's really not that difficult when you understand the dynamics, but lack of knowledge in this area can result in even the most talented designers getting it wrong.

A recently reported case is that of a computer software company, specialising in games, which set up a high street shop. Within the shop they had a section where people could actually come in and play the games first to see if they liked them, and they were puzzled when they didn't get a good response from customers and turnover was low. A colour consultant soon discovered the reason. The decor had been carried out in a futuristic style, using blues and lots of metal. While the concept behind the design was good, it did not have any colours from the warm end of the spectrum, the colours that appeal most to children – and this was the main market for the product. After redecorating using oranges and yellows, the area became a great attraction and business increased as a direct result. This example clearly shows how vital it is for an interior designer to have a good knowledge of colour psychology. While the design concept was good, it did not attract business the way it should have. A better understanding of the subject would have enabled the designer to get it right first time, and they would not have spent money redecorating the interior.

The possibilities for using colour to increase a business's sales and profits are unlimited, and this can literally be applied to any business, whether you are selling a product or a service. Before we go on to examine other ways that colour can make you money, let's look at one more type of business and see how a restaurant could apply colour psychology to increase its profits.

In order for a restaurant to increase sales, it needs a fast turnover of customers. Naturally, the more meals that can be served, the more money can be taken resulting in greater profits. Once again, colour can help tremendously. We have already seen that warm colours, namely oranges and reds, are the best colours to stimulate the appetite, and they are also lively, activating colours which will not encourage people to linger or rest too much after eating. Most successful fast food chains have these colours in their logos and all their packaging.

The whole concept of fast food is to keep staff and customers moving, so that a good turnover will be achieved, however, this same strategy can be applied to any restaurant to increase turnover without making patrons feel 'rushed'. Music, lighting and other accessories can be combined with warm colours to help create a more relaxed mood in a restaurant, and this looks so inviting and welcoming to customers that it is hard to resist. Yet in spite of this, the powerful effect of the colour will cause patrons to believe that they have been in the restaurant longer than they actually have, and encourage them to move on relatively quickly. Clearly, you don't have to look like a fast food restaurant in order to achieve fast turnover and fast profits.

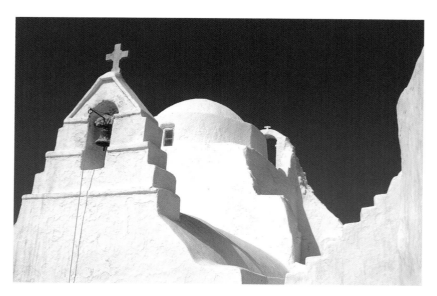

In hot countries, houses are painted white to keep them cool. Using warm colours will have the reverse effect and help the buildings to retain heat.

Reducing overheads

Reducing overheads, as any business owner will know, is the next most important way to increase profits, and once again, colour comes to the rescue. We have already looked in detail at how warm and cool colours work, and how warm colours can actually generate more heat. So why can't we use warm colours in order to reduce heating bills? Well, we can, and in large factories or warehouses that are particularly draughty and difficult to heat, this can save a company hundreds of thousands of pounds per year. A well-known case study is that of a United States factory cafeteria that had light blue walls. The temperature was kept to a steady 72°F, but employees regularly complained of being cold. Even after the temperature was raised to 75°F, some workers continued to wear their coats to meals. A colour consultant recommended the walls be painted coral, after which they began to complain that it was too warm. The temperature was reduced to the original 72°F and everyone was happy. It doesn't take a genius to figure out how this can be of benefit to all of us, in our homes as well as our workplaces. However, in larger companies that have many buildings to heat the results will most certainly be more drastic – as will the savings.

Another way overheads can be reduced is by planning space more effectively so that the amount of actual space needed is less, keeping rental costs to a minimum. Most people think horizontally when it comes to interiors – not laterally. That is, when they want to add something to their interior, they automatically think they need more floor space to accommodate it, and they rarely think of the most effective way of using their existing space. A skilful designer can offer possibilities that you would never think of, and while you may feel that this is not completely relevant to the subject of colour, colour will obviously play an important role maintaining a spacious appearance. This is a good reminder that it is the combination of skills that makes the designer uniquely valuable to the client.

Increasing productivity

Increasing productivity is a more indirect way for a business to increase their profits, but it is also vitally important for business success, and once again, colour can be used to your advantage in a number of ways.

Break times are an important part of our working day, and we all need time to relieve ourselves from the monotony of our jobs, to stretch out our body and recharge our batteries, so to speak. While employers will naturally prefer to have staff working when they feel refreshed and clear-headed, each year companies lose money when workers delay unnecessarily and idle away production time. It is all too easy for people to get caught up in conversation with their co-workers once they have moved away from their workstation, and the challenge is a difficult one for employers. Striking the right balance between providing a pleasant area for staff to take a break, and one that is too comfortable, so they are slow to leave it is not easy, but colour can help.

A novel approach to this problem was taken by a factory owner in the United States, who painted the men's rooms an unpleasant shade of electric green to stop staff loitering. Productivity increased by eight per cent almost overnight, and although there may have been other solutions that would make the owner more favourable with staff, you have to admire his ingenuity. He achieved his objective, and it just goes to prove that there are no rules, only guidelines.

The more usual approach to this type of problem would be to use a strong, activating colour, such as red or orange, which would mean the room was no longer a relaxing 'rest room', but one that would encourage staff to move quickly. There are a number of well-known cases in which colour psychology has been applied in this way to create either a motivating or soothing environment, depending on the requirement. Sports coaches in particular have favoured this approach, including Knute Rockne, the legendary Notre Dame American football coach, who had the locker room of his own team painted red, to stir up the players, and the visiting teams' locker room painted in calming blue-greens, attempting to sedate them before the game and when they were relaxing at half-time. This approach was adopted by so many coaches, particularly in American football, that various sports associations have begun to introduce rules that the visiting teams' locker room cannot be painted a different colour than that of the home team's. In other words, they can be red, blue or any colour of the rainbow, but both locker rooms have to be painted the same colour. Obviously these coaches knew exactly what they were doing when they deliberately selected those colours, but there have been times when these effects have been experienced quite by accident.

Using strong, active colours
creates an energetic mood that
will keep people moving.

For instance, in a newly built prison which had each of its four wings painted in a different colour, the prison governor and his staff soon noticed that the behaviour of the prisoners varied significantly depending on which wing they lived in. Those prisoners that resided in the red and yellow wings of the prison were more inclined towards violent behaviour than those that lived in the blue and green wings. This was obviously a serious mistake for a prison to make, but they seem to be catching on quickly as many prisons now have pink holding cells to reduce violent and aggressive behaviour in prisoners. Caution though, the pink must be pastel, as many shades contain too much red, which will have a stimulating effect.

If we take these lessons back to the business world, surely there are numerous situations when it would be of considerable benefit to create a motivating, energising environment, and likewise other times when it would help to have a more soothing atmosphere. If you would like to fire up your sales team before you send them out to make calls, wouldn't it be helpful to be in the right surroundings with powerful, energetic colours? The important thing to remember is that it would not be a good idea to use such strong colours in areas where people are working all day long, but if you have an area where people are called together for short periods, this could be a very useful strategy. And what about the reverse effect? Are there any areas where a business might find it useful to deliberately create a calm, relaxing environment, such as a customer service area where complaints are handled and staff sometimes have to deal with irate customers? And what about waiting rooms for doctors and dentists? If you are really creative, you will see applications that even go beyond this, as in the following case:

A London factory required workers to move black metal boxes on a daily basis, but they complained regularly about the strain on their backs, and worked at quite a slow pace. Unknown to them, the same boxes were painted a light green one weekend, and soon after the workers were overheard remarking on the improvement with the 'new lightweight' boxes, and how much faster they could work. Creative thinking provided an ingenious solution to a problem for staff and a potentially bigger problem for the employer. Protecting your staff from strain and work-related injury is the duty of every business, and the benefits can be far more than you realise. As well as increasing productivity and business profits, a company will also protect itself from liability claims resulting in loss of revenue and bad publicity. Companies that think they can't afford to invest money in this area will have to think again – the reality is that they can't afford not to.

Reducing liabilities

Most businesses will be subject to liability claims at some point, but those businesses that are dealing with the public on an everyday basis need to be more vigilant than most to ways of safeguarding themselves from this, while naturally protecting the public at large from unnecessary injury. Much of this is common sense, and there are tried and tested choices that will help you to create a safe environment, but there are also some very simple mistakes that seem to occur time and time again.

Take patterns for instance: have you ever come across a really busy, brightly coloured pattern which feels as if it is jumping towards you? When a pattern like this is used on flooring, it is not uncommon for people to perceive the floor as if it was advancing, particularly people whose motor responses are slow due to old age or alcohol intake, and then to fall to the floor. There is a valid reason for mentioning these two categories in particular, as high-traffic areas in hotels and public houses mostly use patterned carpets for practicality as well as comfort. And what about the simple method of using a contrasting colour to mark the edge of a platform and so prevent someone falling or slipping because they didn't see it properly? It really shouldn't be that difficult to get it right first time, but getting it wrong is an expensive mistake that few businesses can afford to make.

Another phenomenon worth investigating is that of 'sick building syndrome', which first appeared in the 1980s, when for some unexplained reason workers in certain environments had higher rates of sickness than usual. In hindsight, many of the reasons are quite clear, and once again colour came to the rescue. In one factory, for instance, where absenteeism was excessive, the lighting was eventually discovered to be the problem as it gave off a bluish cast. This type of lighting actually made people 'look sick', and resulted in workers physically feeling ill. While it was not possible to change the lighting, the simple solution was to paint the walls a warm beige, which counterbalanced the effect of the blue. This obviously had the desired effect, as absenteeism dropped immediately.

Another example is that of a lipstick factory, where female workers were experiencing an unusually high amount of migraines and headaches. Obviously the high absenteeism was costing the company large amounts of money, so they were relieved when it was discovered that the women working there were being overexposed to the colour red, the most powerful colour of the spectrum. By simply painting the walls green to complement and balance the intensity of the red, the headaches were dramatically reduced.

Office workers are also at risk, particularly those that are required to spend a large amount of their time at computer terminals. If the surrounding colours are poorly chosen, office workers will also be prone to headaches and visual fatigue. Care must be taken to avoid colours or fixtures that create glare, as this will create strain on the eyes that could very likely cause impaired vision over a number of years.

Full-time workers spend most of their waking day in their employment, so any improvements in the work environment are hugely welcome and result in a better quality of life all round. The fact that colour can help to improve the quality of life in this way is something that has to be taken advantage of, and even the medical profession (who are noted for their scepticism) have begun to pay attention.

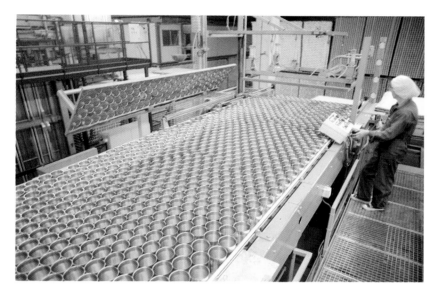

Overexposure to strong colours can be easily rectified by introducing complementary colours to the environment.

Healing green softens the harsh impact of this industrial environment.

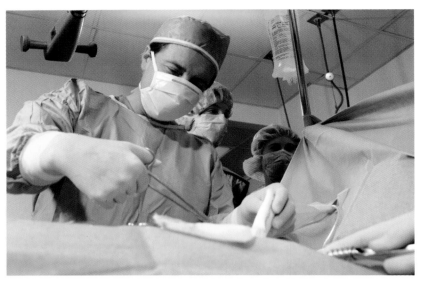

Coloured light is the most common treatment for jaundiced babies. This treatment is also effective for burn victims.

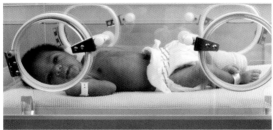

Improving our health and quality of life

As people become more aware of the harmful side effects of prescription drugs and invasive surgery, the search for safer and more effective forms of medical treatment grows stronger. While conventional medicine is based on science, alternative therapies have been built on centuries of intuition, and rather than see them as opposed to each other, we are beginning to see that they are in fact complementary to each other. Colour therapy, which dates back to Egyptian times, uses coloured light to restore balance to the body, and its use is far more common that most people realise, even within mainstream medicine.

Until the 1960s, blood transfusions were given to premature babies suffering from jaundice, which carried high risks and led to many infant deaths. Exposure to white light replaced this treatment, and soon after it was discovered that blue light was, in fact, even more effective. This pain-free method of treatment is now the most common form of treatment for the condition, and it has also been shown to be effective in the treatment of rheumatoid arthritis, and in the treatment of some cancers and skin conditions. Green light, on the other hand, has been used to treat second- and third-degree burns, and burns that are treated in this way have healed far more quickly than normal with a dramatic lessening in pain for the patient. These results are very impressive, but some of the new therapies that are currently being developed are achieving results that are no less than staggering. For instance, Scandinavian physicist Dr Oscar Brunlar was able to reduce the required insulin levels in diabetics from 145 to 25 units by treating patients with yellow-orange light. And in Europe, a new treatment, called colourpuncture, is achieving impressive results, healing an average of 40 per cent of patients that conventional medicine has given up on. Considering the deteriorated state that most of these patients are already in when they begin treatment, this success rate is remarkable indeed.

While the colours that you choose for decorating are obviously not going to cure those suffering from medical conditions, they can help immensely in reducing levels of pain and by shortening recovery times. Kate Baldwin, MD, FACS, former Senior Surgeon of the Women's Hospital, Philadelphia, observed, 'I can produce quicker and more accurate results with colour than with any, or all other methods combined, and with less strain on the patient.' And many hospitals have followed this advice to find that patients placed in blue rooms after major surgery recovered far more quickly than normal. While use of colour in this area is only in its infant stages, the last chapter gives clear guidelines as to which colours are suitable for different situations, and if we really begin to use this information, I believe we shall see some incredible results.

There are many opportunities to apply this knowledge and create supportive surroundings for those that we care about. Professional designers can create even more impact by bringing this to nursing homes, hospitals, and in fact any treatment centre where people are suffering from physical or mental illness. The real question is, why wait until someone has become ill to think about the most supportive colours for their surroundings? Why not use colour now to create the right environment for a full and healthy life, so that it might help us avoid illness and enjoy a better quality of life?

Colour and intelligence

A three-year study in Munich showed that children's IQ could be raised by as much as 12 points when walls were painted certain shades of yellow and orange. The least productive colours, which were white, black, grey and brown, actually caused a drop in IQ. Obviously the wall colour doesn't have some miraculous effect on our brain cells, but in helping to create a more stimulating environment our emotional state is altered, making us more receptive to learning. This has obviously yet to be implemented in schools, as white remains the most popular choice for school walls, but it is clearly unintelligent not to use such a simple tool that can have this much of an impact on the grades of our children. Furthermore, if this is brought into the world of business, surely it can help to create more efficient training courses, possibly reducing training times, and once again saving money.

I trust by now that you are beginning to see how powerful the colours that you choose can be, and how valuable the information in this book is if you apply it correctly. The important thing to remember is that the real value lies in the ability to balance colour psychology with all the other elements of the design.

putting it all together – planning your colour scheme

chapter **10**

Having reached the final chapter, you now have all the information you need to create the perfect colour scheme for any situation, and the knowledge contained within this book, coupled with your own intuition, will help you create outstanding interiors.

The best place to begin is by deciding on the style or look that you wish to create for the room. Do you want a romantic bedroom, an exotic dining room or a modern interior for a hotel lobby? If there are any existing items that have to be incorporated into the scheme, then they have to be taken into account at this stage. Very few people will have the luxury of refurbishing their entire home from scratch, and even then, there may be items of furniture or certain accessories that they wish to incorporate into the scheme. Very often, designers will be asked to make use of existing curtains or carpets, which are obviously expensive to replace, and this may decide on the overall design direction. While it is possible to adapt many pieces to fit a certain style, there are times when it won't work. For instance, a heavily patterned Axminster carpet probably won't suit a contemporary style, and in situations like this, choices have to be made – either change the style to incorporate the carpet successfully, or scrap the carpet and find something more appropriate. This part of the process does need a bit of ruthlessness, and if you are designing for someone else, you may need to be a little forceful. Once you have an idea of how you want the room to look, then you can begin to select the individual items you need to create it.

Successful interior designers are confident with their interior schemes, because most of them don't begin to decorate until they can see in their mind's eye exactly how the room will look once it has been completed. Once they have that vision, it is easy for them to decide which items will work and which won't, because they already know the style, colours and type of furnishings that will be most suitable. There may be one or two changes along the way to accommodate availability of items and the designer must be slightly flexible in this regard, but the overall impression will be maintained. To help you narrow down your choices and really see which items will work best together, taking the time to create a sample or mood-board is one of the most worthwhile exercises that you can do.

The sample board will help you to be sure that patterns and colours co-ordinate, as it literally helps to create a mini-version of the decor scheme and gives you a sneak preview as to how the colours and style will work together. It is also a creative exercise in itself, and the process of putting together a sample board will often generate ideas for those perfect finishing touches that give the real 'designer look'. The most obvious benefit is that you can see all this before you commit yourself to buying anything, and therefore you avoid making expensive mistakes.

For designers, a sample or mood-board is also a very useful tool, which can help you instil confidence in your clients. Generally, people employ an interior designer because they don't trust themselves to get it right. Just because they are paying a designer doesn't necessarily give them any more confidence, particularly in residential design, when you are dealing with their homes. A sample board will help them somewhat to see the direction that you are taking them, and will hopefully help to 'sell' them your idea and your professionalism. This is so important, as a client that is unsure can be indecisive and can delay a job from progressing if they don't have the confidence.

So how do you go about creating your own sample board?

Strictly speaking, a sample board should contain actual samples of the wallcovering or paints, and carpets, fabrics, etc. that you intend to use in the room. However, it can be quite difficult to find brochures of the furniture that you intend using, and then even when you do, the illustration may be out of all proportion to the other elements on your board. This is also true of accessories and lighting, etc. One way around this is to choose similar styles and colours from other brochures and magazines, and even to look for pictures that show a finished room in a style similar to the one you wish to create. When I am making up boards, I will also include pictures that depict a mood or feeling, which I feel is a source of inspiration for the room. For example, if I was creating an analogous scheme using blues and greens, I might attach a postcard to my board showing green mountains against a blue sky, to suggest the calm, tranquil mood that I would be striving to create by using these colours. For this reason, I always refer to my boards as mood-boards, and I explain to clients that they are merely a tool to help them visualise the way the elements will work together, and the overall mood or effect that will be achieved. It doesn't mean, however, that the fireplace shown on the board for example, is the exact one that I will be installing in their room.

Whichever approach you prefer to take, here are some tips to help you create a successful presentation:

Place your fabric swatches, paint and flooring samples, etc. on your board in the same proportions as they will be used in the room. This is the real key to helping you make the right decisions, as your board will help you to judge if the colours and proportions will work.

If you have trouble getting samples from shops or suppliers, take note of the reference codes and request a sample directly from the manufacturer. Most will be happy to oblige, and the delay is usually minimal.

Fabrics and wallpaper samples that have large patterns can be used on the board to check for colour compatibility, but the overall effect of the pattern will be hard to represent clearly. If this is an issue, reduce the pattern on a colour photocopier to see how it relates to the other elements in the room. (Be aware that the colour reproduction of copying will not be totally accurate, but this is a good way to check how your pattern will work if you are at all unsure.)

Paint swatches can be small and make minimal impact on your board. One way around this is to have a tester pot made up and to paint a piece of thick white card with the colour. Once it has dried, cut it to the appropriate proportions and stick it directly to the sample or mood-board.

If you are using existing furnishings in a room, represent their colour on the board by matching up paint swatches or taking a small sample if possible.

If you are creating a sample board rather than a mood-board, try to follow a logical sequence for your layout. For instance, place flooring samples near the bottom of the board, and ceiling lighting near the top etc. In either case, experiment with the layout of your samples to achieve an effect which is visually pleasing to the eye before sticking the samples to your board.

Use spraymount adhesive or double-sided sticky tape to secure samples to the board itself. For large bulky items, such as carpet, you might use velcro pads to attach them to the board. This way they can also be removed for transportation to avoid damage.

Get as many samples as you can for any project. For example, if you can't decide between a yellow or orange wall colour, get samples of both. Once you begin to experiment with the layout of your board, it will quickly become clear which samples work best together, and you will be surprised how many of your choices are eliminated in no time at all.

Try to use your board to represent the style of the room as well as the colour choices. For instance, if you have decided on a fuss-free, contemporary scheme, don't clutter the board with too many accessories or items. Try to keep some open space, the same way that you would in the room itself.

Likewise, use pictures of accessories to add character to your board in the same way that you would use them in any room. It can be really interesting and fun to add textured items such as feathers, leaves or even sweets for a child's room. Remember that they are just accessories, and don't let them take over the board.

For the most part, pictures should have clean edges on them by cutting with a craft knife against a metal ruler. Use manicure scissors to cut small, awkwardly shaped pictures, so that you can cut right up to the edge of the picture. Poorly cut pictures will be highlighted once they are placed on to the board, and they will give an untidy look to your presentation. (Keeping this point in mind, there are times when using torn cuttings and frayed edges of fabric can help to create an artistic and creative looking board, but this must be in keeping with the style of the room. This type of approach would not be suitable for a classic Georgian interior.)

Look for pictures in books and magazines that show the style or look that you are trying to achieve. Take colour photocopies if you want to hold on to your originals.

If you are creating a board for a client, remember to use a title block so that they clearly understand which room the board represents. You can include small captions on the board which explain its function and the reasons for some of the choices, and if you decide to do this just remember to keep it brief and don't let them spoil the effect of your board. Alternatively, include a short design brief separately to explain your choices and the purpose of the board itself.

By building up the elements of your room on a small scale at first, you will quickly spot anything out of place and avoid expensive mistakes. If you haven't already decided on which accessories to use in your scheme, the creative process of building your board will usually inspire you right down to the last detail, so that you know exactly which finishing touches you require. These are the unique elements to an interior that give a complete and professional finish, and they are equally important in creating unity throughout your scheme. Accessories are often the last items to be selected, so it is appropriate then that we finish off by looking at a variety of finishing touches and how they can help to tie your scheme together.

Finishing touches and accessories

Finishing touches and accessories will breathe life into an interior, and without them a room will generally feel as if something is missing or that it is not quite finished. On the other hand, there are times when most of us have been in rooms where we have spotted items that are clearly misplaced, detracting from the overall scheme and from the individual item itself. This is really the effect of simultaneous contrast where an otherwise attractive piece can look awkward or clumsy simply because it is in the wrong setting. There's no doubt about it, pictures, ornaments, and knick-knacks all go a long way to creating a finished look, but they need just as much thought as any other element within the design.

Accessorising a room is a skill in itself and one that every designer should cultivate. Accessories allow you as an individual to put your own stamp on an interior, and include something that you identify with to make that scheme your own. Even in corporations, they have their own personality, and finishing touches that incorporate elements of company logos and colours can play a critical role in establishing the corporate identity and overall look. Most importantly, accessories play an important part in achieving continuity and unity throughout a scheme. They can even help to rescue a mistake, by restoring balance and harmony to a colour scheme. So let's examine some of the choices available and look at the most effective ways of using them to create unity in your scheme.

Pictures

Pictures are one of the most common ways to add a finishing touch to walls and to inject a little individuality to the overall scheme, but they can also play a major role in tying your colour scheme together and creating unity throughout the room or interior. Obviously the picture itself and the style and colours contained within it should be in keeping with the rest of the interior, but the type of frame you use (if indeed you do opt for one) will also play an important part in the complete look. Think carefully about using a mount inside the frame. These are some of the smaller details that most people just don't think about, but they can have a major impact on your scheme. The colour of a mount is very important, and in fact you can combine colours by using double and triple mounts sometimes. In addition to this, mounts can be cut to unusual shapes, and the pictures can also be offset which can create a striking effect. It is also possible to use fabric as a mount, thereby adding pattern or texture as well as colour, and linking it to other areas of the room such as curtains or tablecloths, bed linen, etc.

If a picture has provided the starting point for your decor scheme, then you don't have to worry too much about it matching perfectly, but if you are trying to find something suitable, it can take forever to find the exact picture you want that is the right colour, style and size for your particular scheme. One way around this is to use mounts and frames to increase the overall size of a picture if you have something that is too small. Another alternative is to maybe use small pictures but to hang them in groups, so that visually the effect appears much larger. But what if you can't find a picture that you feel ties in with the scheme? Always remember, colour is the key, and rather than leave a bare wall until such time as you find the perfect piece, use colour in the form of paint, wallpaper or fabric to create unity throughout the room. A simply framed block of colour can work wonderfully, or it can even be a number of colours combined in an abstract form. Once the colour is right and the style doesn't conflict with the rest of the room, then the end result will work.

Another clever trick is to use the actual wall space behind the picture to highlight and define the picture itself in a complementary colour. It is easy to create unity in a scheme this way, by literally drawing colour around the room, and it is also a useful trick if you have a picture that is a little too small for the area. By painting a larger panel for the picture to be placed on, you are visually enlarging the picture and making the size more appropriate for the room. This can also be used to create a more uniform shape for displaying unusually shaped items such as ethnic masks or personal collections of unusual items.

Collections and unusual items

Collections and unusual items can be used as wall
hangings to really give a unique flavour to an interior,
but they have to be handled carefully if they are to work
in harmony with the entire scheme and not take over the
show completely. Examples of suitable items would be
plates, African masks, Oriental fans or even decorative
items of clothing. Obviously the colours must be
harmonious with the rest of the interior, but you also
have to be careful not to create a display that is too
busy and distracting, thereby detracting from the overall
room. Collections of many pieces can have this effect,
but by using the same trick of painting one large panel
on the wall behind several smaller pieces, visually we
perceive a more unified picture. This can also be used to
create balance amongst a variety of oddly shaped
objects, as the background panel will generally have a
more uniform shape. If there are variations in colour
throughout the collection, then this can be a very
effective way of linking them not only with each other,
but with the rest of the room as well. There are many
possibilities, but you have to be willing to experiment a
little to get the effect you require and avoid overkill.

In our houses we tend to be more conservative with our
choice of accessories, but thinking about this just
slightly differently can present a wonderful way of
expressing your individuality and really creating a
unique effect into the bargain. In commercial interiors,
using accessories in this way can help to project the
company's image or personality most effectively. Think
about the international chain of Hard Rock Cafés, for
instance, which use paraphernalia from the music
industry to adorn their walls, and everything from
leather jackets to motorbikes in the centre of the floor.
Large offices and institutional buildings tend to stick to
a straightforward, no-nonsense approach to decorating
their interiors, but every company has its own
personality. If you are involved in designing for such
buildings, decorating the building with items that reflect
the company's personality will not only reinforce their
corporate image, but it will generally create a more
pleasant environment for staff and customers alike.

Ornaments and art pieces

Ornaments and art pieces can also be displayed on
walls by fixing or hanging them directly in some cases,
or by displaying them on shelves, either individually or
in groups. More commonly though, we use a variety of
ornaments and sculptures to add style details and
balance to the overall scheme, by placing them in
strategic positions around the room, on top of coffee
tables and mantelpieces, etc. One thing to keep in mind
about ornaments is that they tend to multiply without us
noticing, and most of us accumulate a huge number of
them throughout the years. Where we may have started
with a fairly minimal scheme, before we know it the style
of the room can look almost Victorian because we have
collected too many knick-knacks. Once we have parted
with money for them, we can be reluctant to let them go,
and while the finishing touches are so important, having
too much can often be worse than having none at all.
You must be ruthless if you want to create a scheme
that will work, and each piece that goes into the room
must be objectively assessed as to how it will work with
all the other elements. If it doesn't work, either use it in
another room or get rid of it completely.

Soft furnishings and curtains

Soft furnishings and curtains play such an important part in any interior, but in residential design they can make or break your scheme as they really can help to pull a room together. If you are having curtains made to order, it is always worth ordering slightly more fabric than needed and think about using it in the following ways to help co-ordinate your scheme and provide continuity of colour and pattern around the room:

In the dining room, the same fabric can be used with wadding to create placemats, napkins or to trim a tablecloth. The obvious method of creating a matching tablecloth can look a little contrived, but by adding a simple trim or napkins, unity can be achieved without overkill.

In the kitchen, placemats again can be used, or padded cushions for chairs or benches. Using the same fabric to create oven gloves, and to trim tea towels and aprons, giving a subtle designer touch to the whole scheme.

Bedrooms are one of the most popular places for people to use co-ordinated fabrics, particularly matching duvet sets with curtains. However, by ordering an upholstered headboard and possibly a valance sheet to match the curtains, the scheme will still be co-ordinated, but the effect will generally be subtler. A practical point to consider if you do choose duvets with matching curtain fabric, is that duvet covers will fade with washing, and where it probably wouldn't be noticeable if they were on their own, they will quickly begin to look faded beside the curtains.

Using cushions and draped tablecloths is another obvious way of pulling colour together throughout the room. You should also think about combining fabrics with plain contrasts to add more visual interest and avoid too much repetition and overkill.

Lastly, some fabrics are so interesting in their own right that they can even be framed, in whole or in part, as artwork for the walls. Very detailed designs can often provide three or four co-ordinating pictures for a room that can look wonderful with a good mount and frame. The actual curtain fabric itself usually hangs in pleats, so the full details of the design are not always apparent to the eye.

Using fabric in this way doesn't necessarily mean overkill, but you must judge each situation on its own individual merits.

Plants and flowers

Plants and flowers are equally important for adding colour to your scheme and for restoring the balance of nature in your interior. They prevent a room from looking too sterile and they often add scent as well as visual appeal. With the variety of plants available, there are some wonderful textures and shapes to tease your senses, and even in areas where there is no natural light, consider using artificial plants, some of which are very effective. In offices and commercial buildings, one worry can be regarding who will care for the plants, but there are a number of companies who will lease plants, and the rental company themselves will often be responsible for the maintenance of the plants.

Decorating the wall directly

Decorating the wall directly is probably one of the most versatile options available, as it allows you to choose the exact colour, style and scale or size to suit the scheme and the area. This can be done using a variety of techniques, including stencils, découpage and even freehand painting. For instance, if you were trying to create an Oriental theme in your home or indeed in a Chinese restaurant, why not have Chinese lettering painted directly on to the walls in the exact size and colour that you need. This is a very simple, inexpensive way to achieve unity throughout a scheme, which takes just a little planning and forethought.

This method can be particularly useful in very small areas, as the 'accessory' is flush with the wall, rather than projecting from it, even if it is only a small amount. By actually painting a picture directly on to the wall, you can add contrasting colour and still accessorise the room without taking up any valuable space. This can even be carried further by painting a mural or *trompe l'oeil*, when the three-dimensional painting will visually open up the area and effectively double or even triple the size.

Another instance when this type of decoration is particularly useful is when you are dealing with walls that aren't straight, such as those in an attic or dormer bungalow. In these instances, it is not possible to hang a picture against a wall, but using this paint technique or découpage is a great way to add those essential finishing touches. For me, the real beauty of using this type of decoration is that you are not buying something manufactured, instead you are creating something completely unique. Not only does this give you a one-off interior, but it also allows you to have complete control over the scale, balance and, most importantly, the colour.

Essentials

Essentials are those necessary items that play an important part in our everyday living, but that don't always complement the decor that we have worked so hard to achieve. The likes of cleaning products would come under this category. After all, we need to have detergents, air fresheners, shampoos and soaps, yet often the packaging, that is designed to stand out on supermarket shelves, stands out a little too much in our home environments. Very often bleaches and washing powders will be hidden away in a cupboard under the sink, but what about products that may be visible in the bathroom, such as shampoos or cleansers? How do we prevent them from making our scheme look untidy, and from clashing with the colours that we have chosen for our decor?

The solution to this problem is really quite obvious, but in everyday practice so few people pay attention to these final details. For instance, in the bathroom, choose soap and toilet roll that match the room. Shampoos and other toiletries come in some great packages, and if they don't, put them into glass containers or others that do match your scheme. You may see this as taking it all a little too far, but this is what makes the difference between a nice interior and an outstanding interior.

There are many hardware items that also fall into this category, and likewise, all it takes is a little extra thought to ensure that even your essentials can play a part in your scheme co-ordinating. For instance, why not choose stainless steel pots and pans for your kitchen, and a chrome pedal bin, rather than just a functional plastic swing bin. Or a plain wooden chopping board, rather than the strongly coloured option that will fight for attention with other items in the kitchen. In this way, you are not just choosing functional items, but pieces that will also act as accessories to your entire scheme. Even food itself, such as biscuits, coffee and tea, can be stored in see-through jars or other attractive containers to add interesting colour and texture to the scheme.

In our workplaces too, there are many opportunities to think about those final details. Office filing trays and pencil holders all add colour to your overall scheme, but if you don't control this seemingly small aspect of the design, before you know it there is an unharmonious mixture of colour that looks untidy and causes distraction.

Giving attention to these seemingly small details is what helps to create a truly professional finish to your interior. These are the real finishing touches that make a room truly impressive, and with a little forethought you can get full potential out of every item that goes into your home and working environments.

Conclusion

Colour is my passion, and I hope that having got to this point in the book, you have caught that passion and will experience the fun and pleasure of adding colour to your world and the world of those around you. While many people still see colour as frivolous and something of an afterthought, that view is changing as we take a more holistic approach towards life in general and begin to realise the important role that colour plays in our health and happiness. I hope that you will join me in my quest to put a little colour out there, so that we can all benefit from environments that support us, wherever we are in life.

I would like to leave you with a final thought that is a little romantic but holds great appeal for me. During his investigations into colour, Sir Isaac Newton made a comparison between the musical scale and the colours of the rainbow, and indeed he went on to ascribe a musical note to each colour. For the last few hundred years, work has been continuing to create a musical instrument that is able to 'play' colours, and there are many similarities between the colours of the rainbow and the notes of the musical scale. In the same way that so many pieces of music can be created with only seven notes, the possibilities with colour are similarly infinite. When singers match their voices and sing in unison, although each singer sings in his or her own key, they harmonise. This is harmony in song and the same principle applies to colour harmony. So whether you prefer a dramatic opera or an easy listening ballad, use colour to write your own music – who knows, you may create a symphony.

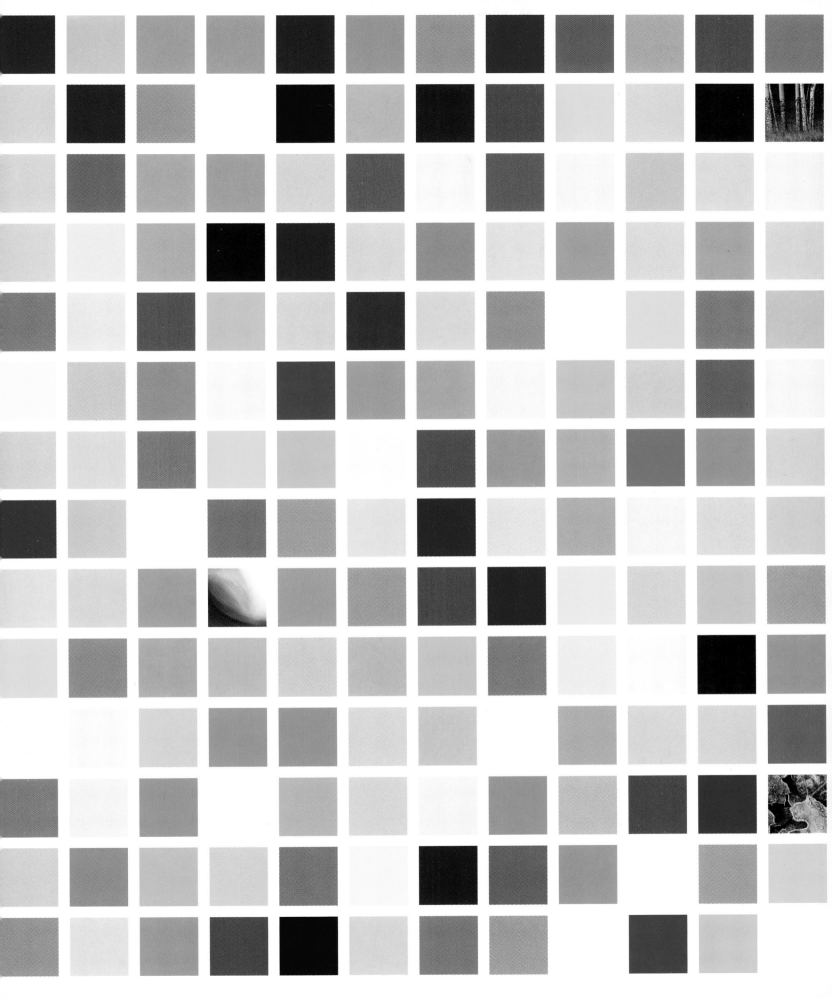

Glossary

Achromatic Black, white and neutral greys

Additive colour Colour created by mixing light

Analogous colours Colours which lie beside each other on the colour wheel

Chroma The strength or purity of a colour. For instance, a bright, pure blue or a dull, greyed blue

Chromatic Containing colour – that is, any colour, other than black, white and grey which is achromatic

Colour harmony Achieved when the colours are balanced and harmonise with each other, rather than contrast in a negative way

Colour notation A systematic way of describing colour so that the same colours can be reproduced accurately

Colour psychology The scientific study of colour and its subsequent effect on our moods and emotions

Colour temperature The ability of a colour to reflect heat. Reds, oranges and yellows are regarded as warm colours, whereas blues, greens and purples are generally regarded as cool

Colour wheel A segmented circle (rather like a pie chart) which shows the relationships between colours

Complementary colours Colours which lie directly opposite each other on the colour wheel

Electromagnetic radiation A form of energy, of which visible light and colour is a small part

Hue A pure colour as represented on the colour wheel

Mood-board A display board that contains pictures and colours suggestive of a specific mood that will be created by a particular scheme. It may also contain actual samples to be used in the scheme

Monochromatic colour Colour of a single hue

Munsell colour system A widely used colour system which identifies all colours by the three dimensions of hue, value and chroma

Neutral colours Theoretically speaking, the only true neutral colours are achromatic. In everyday practice, however, this term refers to 'natural' colours such as beige, brown, cream, stone and grey

Pastel A colour created by mixing a pure hue with a neutral grey

Primaries Colours that cannot be created by mixing other colours. The primary colours are yellow, blue and red

Sample board A tool used by interior designers that features actual samples of the various materials to be used in an interior scheme. Sometimes referred to as a mood-board

Saturation The strength or intensity of a colour

Secondaries Colours created by mixing primaries. The secondary colours are green, orange and purple

Shade A colour created by mixing black with a pure hue

Simultaneous contrast The apparent ability of a colour to change its appearance or effect when it is placed beside another colour

Spectrum The band of colours contained within white light. When white light is directed through a prism, the colours of the spectrum can be clearly seen as they appear in order of their wavelength: red, orange, yellow, green, blue, indigo and violet

Subtractive colour Colour created by mixing pigment

Tertiaries Colours created by mixing primary and secondary colours together according to their position on the colour wheel

Tetrad colours Four hues which are found at equal distances from each other on the colour wheel

Tint A colour created by mixing white with a pure hue

Tone The lightness or darkness of a colour. Also known as value

Triad colours Three hues which are found at equal distances from each other on the colour wheel

Value The degree of lightness or darkness in a colour. More commonly referred to as tone

Useful Reading

The Art of Colour Johannes Itten,
Van Nostrand Reinhold (1969)

The Beginner's Guide to Colour Psychology
Angela Wright, Kyle Cathie Ltd (1995)

*Colour Me Healing: Colourpuncture: A New Medicine
of Light* Jack Allanach, Element (1997)

Colour Perception Tim Armstrong,
Tarquin Publications (1991)

Colour Psychology And Colour Therapy Faber Birren,
Citadel Press (1950)

Colourscape Michael Lancaster,
Academy Editions (1996)

Discover The Magic of Colour Lillian Verner Bonds,
Optima (1993)

Healing With Colour Helen Graham,
Gill & Macmillan (1996)

Light: Medicine of The Future Jacob Liberman,
Bear & Company (1991)

The Luscher Colour Test Dr Max Luscher,
Random House (1969)

Principles of Colour Faber Birren,
Van Nostrand Reinhold (1969)

Relativity And Quantum Physics Roger Muncaster,
Stanley Thornes Ltd (1995)

Theory of Colours Johann Wolfgang van Goethe,
MIT Press (1970)

The author, editor and publisher would like to thank the following for use of their images in this book:

Ideal Standard
The Bathroom Works
National Avenue
Kingston upon Hull
HU5 4HS
United Kingdom

Harlequin Fabrics & Wallcoverings Limited
Ladybird House
Beeches Road
Loughborough
Leicestershire
LE11 2HA
United Kingdom
For information on any products shown, visit their website at www.harlequin.uk.com

Next Home
Next Retail Limited
Desford Road
Enderby
Leicester
LE9 5AT
United Kingdom
Products illustrated are from their Autumn/Winter 2000 collection. For more information telephone +44 (0)116 2866411

Dulux
Shandwick International
43 King Street
Covent Garden
London, WC2E 8RJ
United Kingdom
For information on any products shown, visit their website at www.shandwick.com

Monkwell
10–12 Wharfdale Road
Bournemouth, BH4 9BT
United Kingdom
For information on any products shown, visit their website at www.monkwell.com or telephone in the UK on +44 (0)1202 752944 or in the USA please contact Lee Jofa +1 516 752 7600

Crowson – Fabrics, Furnishings & Wallcoverings
Crowson House
Bellbrook Park
Uckfield
East Sussex
TN22 1QZ
United Kingdom
For information on any products shown, visit their website at www.crowsonfabrics.com or telephone on +44 1825 761055 or fax on +44 1825 764283

Qualceram
Unit A, Merrywell Business Park
Ballymount
Dublin 12
Ireland
Telephone +353 (0)1 450 0595

Focus Lighting, Inc.
255 West 101St street,
New York,
NY 10025
Telephone +1 212 865 1565 fax +1 212 865 4217

Stiff and Trevillion
4 Westbourne Grove Mews
London, W11 2RU
United Kingdom
*Telephone +44 (0)20 7299 7100 fax +44 (0)20 7229
7004 e-mail mail@stiff-trevillion.demom.co.uk*
Photographer Morley Von Sternberg

Edinburgh Lighting Design
Jonathan Speirs & Associates Ltd.
Weel Court Hall
Dean Village
Edinburgh, EH4 3BE
Telephone +44 (0)131 226 4474 fax +44 (0)131 220 5331
Photographer Gavin Fraser

McDonald's Rest. Ltd
11–59 High Road
East Finchley
London, N2 8AW
United Kingdom
*Telephone +44 (0)20 8700 7244 fax +44 (0)20 8700
7059*

Chas Krider
219 King Avenue
Columbus
Ohio 43201
USA
Telephone +1 614 299 9709 fax +1 614 299 9797
e-mail chasray@ee.net

Mike Stoane lighting
78 Albion Road
Edinburgh, EH7 5QZ
Telephone +44 (0)131 467 7600 fax +44 (0)131 478 0564
Photographer Kevin Mclean

Also thanks to Therese Coughlan, Nicole Coyne and Orla
Clarke for allowing us to use their sample boards in
Chapter 10.